DIGGING FOR GENEALOGICAL TREASURE

in New England Town Records

Ann Smith Lainhart

New England Historic Genealogical Society

Boston   1996

Library of Congress Cataloging-in-Publication Data.

Lainhart, Ann Smith.

Digging for genealogical treasure in New England town records / Ann Smith
Lainhart.
Includes bibliographical references and index.

1. New England--Genealogy--Archival resources--Directories.
2. Municipal government--New England--Records and correspondence--
Directories.
I. New England Historic Genealogical Society. II. Title.

ISBN 0-88082-053-5
F3.L35 1996
929'.1'02574--dc20   96-8488
                                                                          CIP

Table of Contents

List of Illustrations

Preface

In 1985 I conducted a Saturday workshop at the New England Historic Genealogical Society on New England town records as part of a series of workshops organized by Melinde Lutz Sanborn. Since that time I have lectured both locally and nationally on "New England Town Records: Beyond the Vital Records" and "New England Poor Records." This book has grown out of these lectures.

I would especially like to express my thanks to Jane Fletcher Fiske who also lectures on New England town records and has allowed me to incorporate many of her ideas into this book. She also worked closely with me on an earlier version of the book and has supplied most of the Rhode Island examples.

I also want to thank several people who have read various versions of this book and have offered me examples that they have found in town records. These include Melinde Lutz Sanborn, Lois Ware Thurston, Scott Bartley, Ruth Wilder Sherman, Robert J. Dunkle, Mary Pat Brigham, Jerome Anderson, and Roger D. Joslyn.

Margaret F. Costello designed the book's format and selected most of the illustrations. Shawna Grimm Hansen prepared the indexes.

Ann Smith Lainhart

Introduction

In New England the primary local-level governmental body is the town. While some records are kept on the county or district level — and this varies from state to state — most local records are kept by the town. Except for far northern Maine, there is no land in New England that is not within the bounds of a town or city. This book covers records from the 17th, 18th, and 19th centuries and while there were several incorporated cities in New England by the end of the 19th century, the term "town" could still be applied to them. Therefore, in this book "town" has been used exclusively.

Any researcher working on New England families is aware that most towns kept good records of the births, marriages, and deaths of their inhabitants. The value of these vital records cannot be overestimated, but too many researchers stop after using them, unaware of the wealth of historical and genealogical information to be found in other types of town records. The purpose of this book is to acquaint researchers with what may be found beyond vital records in various town halls in New England.

Town records are definitely the most overlooked source of biographical information on New Englanders. While there were some laws governing what records were to be kept by the towns, researchers will find that each town tended to be somewhat idiosyncratic; the record-keeping in any particular town may even have changed with each new town clerk. This book contains sections on each of the main categories in which researchers are likely to find records: Selectmen or Council minutes, town officers, treasurer's records, tax and assessor records, land records, licenses, ear or cattle marks, manumissions, chattell mortgage books, military records, poor records, and more. So while it is impossible to guarantee that information can be found on any particular individual, the chances are that most male inhabitants of a town will be mentioned in the town records in some way.

The largest section of this book is devoted to the records of poor people. It is in these records that the researcher is most likely to find biographical and genealogical information, especially valuable because these people do not appear in the more widely used probate and land records. Each town took seriously its responsibility to care for its recognized inhabitants, and to document the measures taken on their behalf. The poor are found in many types of records, from treasurer's books to 19th century letters written by overseers of the poor. Almost every family has at least one member who fell on hard times, was wounded or injured, ended up aged and alone, or in some way needed the help of the town. It is well worth the time to search the town records for these people.

Some town records have been published and are thus easier to access and read than the original manuscript volumes. Most other town records still must be used on microfilm or in the town clerk's office. It is hoped that more will be published as the value of these records becomes more apparent, and increased numbers of researchers use them. Certainly the last few years have seen an increased interest in publishing records of definite, if less obvious, genealogical value, such as warnings out, ear marks, and apprenticeships. Nevertheless, there is still a great deal of information buried in the records of New England towns.

DIGGING FOR GENEALOGICAL TREASURE

in New England Town Records

Chapter One

Getting Acquainted with
New England Town Records

Any historian or genealogist who neglects to study town records in the colonial period is running the risk of missing some of the most intimate detail about New Englanders that he is likely to find anywhere. Even well into the 1800s, the town represented a small welfare state, linking the individual and his family with the larger units of government on the county, colony, or state level. For people who owned property and left wills, one can often trace movements and progeny reasonably well using probate and land records, but for the poor, town records are often the only source of information.

From the earliest days of the New England colonies, town government prevailed, carried over from the English system of record-keeping within the parish. On this side of the Atlantic, where church and state were separate, the records were kept by the town clerk rather than the parish clerk as had been the case in England. Each town clerk was elected, along with other town officials, in a meeting of the freemen or inhabitants of his town, called, logically enough, a town meeting. It was his task to keep track of the different kinds of records that were generated by the town government. In this book, many kinds of town records will be discussed, but the reader should keep in mind that the specific records found within each town will vary. Even within a particular town, as the town clerk changed, the types of records which were kept may differ. It is also unfortunate that some town books have been lost or destroyed during the years.

It was recognized in the very beginning that the records should be kept in book form, and often the first item found in a record book is the amount of the payment made for it out of the town treasury. Some books begin with a copy of the town charter, often followed by a list of the first proprietors or settlers there. Because it was not uncommon for a town to be founded by a group of people from an older settlement, the first few meetings may have actually been held in the parent community, and duly noted in the new town's record book.

It is important to be aware of the geographical evolution of towns in New England. As new areas became populated, they were set off as separate towns; searching records for any particular location may involve looking in the records of more than one town. A good guide to the dates of establishment of New England towns, and names of parent towns from which new ones were set off, is provided in Marcia Wiswall Lindberg's *Genealogist's Handbook for New England Research* (third edition, Boston: NEHGS, 1993).

Considering the precarious state of life in the first years of the colonies, it is not surprising that one often finds all kinds of records jumbled together in town record books. The researcher must be prepared to sort out and decipher various records of several types of events in the colonial town, often not in chronological order. The colonial laws simply instructed the town clerks to keep records of births, marriages, deaths, and a record of each man's house and lands; but beyond that it was up to the individual towns to determine what they recorded. While some generalizations can be made, the books of each town will be unique to that town. In Rhode Island, for instance, records of the town council meetings are interspersed with those of the probate court, for the latter was a function of the first and the councilmen simply changed their hats to handle probate business. It is common to find a deed or two in the earliest books, and rare is the town council book of that period that does not contain at least a few records of births, marriages, or deaths. For the sake of economy, every blank space was usually filled, with no attention whatever to chronology, thus adding to the variety. In many Maine towns the warrants and minutes of each town meeting may begin at the top of a new page. Empty space left at the bottom of the previous page might be filled in at a later date with vital records.

Most early records are unindexed. One may be lucky enough to find a transcript for which an index has been made, or a volume which has been briefly indexed with an indication of which pages contain a particular kind of record. Although the original handwriting may be difficult to read, the researcher is helped by the fact that town clerks usually were re-elected year after year and thus the hand did not change too frequently.

Today the office of the town clerk is usually found in a building set aside as the town hall or town house, but for many years before such buildings existed, the town clerk kept his records in his own home. Even today, in many of the smaller New England towns, the town clerk may still conduct business at home with very limited hours. Often the older records are not kept in the physical possession of the clerk, but may be stored for safety in a local bank vault. It is always best, therefore, to call or write in advance to make an appointment to use the records. When writing, define the dates to be searched, as some records have been lost or burned. Current lists of town clerks and their addresses are available from the Secretary of State's Office in each state. For Maine, check also the State Archives publication, *Public Record Repositories in Maine*.

Because a town's vital records are most often in demand, the books containing town meeting and town council records have frequently received less attention and care. The genealogist or historian seeking them is faced with the paradox that most town clerks, involved in the present day business of their office and thus not very knowledgeable about the old books, do nonetheless take their custodianship very seriously. Many are extremely reluctant to allow researchers to handle them. Reasons given may range from concern for the old bindings to a different type of fear, expressed by one town clerk in western Massachusetts, who at first refused to retrieve the books from the basement because "they are full of creepy, crawly things." Most town clerks feel that the records must remain in the town hall building, and efforts to deposit them in archives for safekeeping and ease of access have not often been successful.

Many towns, however, have undertaken to protect and preserve their old records. Several Rhode Island towns have had their early record books repaired and restored. North Kingstown lost many of its records to fire over a century ago, but some that were burned only around the edges have now been restored and appear as ovals of manuscript surrounded by the frame of the page — tantalizing the reader with what must have once been legible there. Wells, Maine, has made very good bound copies of their older town books, thus providing the researcher with access to the records while limiting the use of the original books. Gloucester, Massachusetts, has supported a volunteer committee which aims to organize that town's records into an archive. In the course of this organization, apprenticeship records were found for 373 children bound out between 1739-1852. These have now been abstracted and published.[1]

Before heading directly for a town hall, check to see whether the records may be available in print, in manuscript, or in microform in a library or archive. Most researchers are familiar with the set of printed vital records of Massachusetts towns, but do not realize that many town records are also in print. Appendix A at the end of this book consists of a bibliography of New England town records in print or typescript. One should bear in mind, however, that the transcripts in print may include only the selectmen's or council records. The town clerk may hold still other volumes, such as tax or assessor's books, poor books, school books, records of the town's militia, and more, that will often provide added information.

Other records may be found in manuscript and typescript copies made by researchers and genealogists and deposited in libraries and archives such as the New England Historic Genealogical Society. The public library of Reading, Massachusetts, for instance, has a typescript of early selectmen's records, as well as the records of the First Church of Reading. The library in Concord, Massachusetts, has a collection of abstracts of that town's early records. One should search also in collections catalogued under other names; for example, the original manuscript of the Proprietors' records for the Pocasset Purchase (encompassing present day Tiverton, Rhode Island, and parts of Freetown and Fall River, Massachusetts) is in the Pardon Gray Seabury Collection at the New Bedford Free Public Library.

The New Hampshire State Library houses the largest collection of manuscript town records in New England. Early in the twentieth century, the Library borrowed volumes from most New Hampshire towns and made manuscript copies — over 200 were completed. In most cases the original volumes were then returned to the towns. The manuscripts have since been microfilmed. An every-name index on 3 by 5 inch cards was made, arranged alphabetically by surname and first name, and then alphabetically by the towns in which that name is found. The volume and page number for each occurrence of that name is also noted on the card, sometimes followed by FR (family record) to denote a birth record, or MR (marriage record) to denote a marriage. The nature of other references is not noted on the index cards. For example, the name John Stark appears in the towns of Atkinson, Bedford, Bristol, Canterbury, Conway, Dunbarton, Durham, Epping, Hill, Hollis, Hopkinton, Peterboro, Plainfield, Richmond, Wear, and Westmoreland, while the name Daniel Gillingham appears in only six towns: Bradford, Claremont, Newbury, New London, Sunapee, and Sutton.

A great number of New England town records have been microfilmed by the Church of Jesus Christ of Latter-day Saints, which then gave each town a microfilm copy of its own records. Unfortunately, however, many towns do not have microfilm readers. Some town clerks have been persuaded to give their film to the local library or, as is the case in Boxford, Massachusetts, to the local archives center, which, however, may be open only one day every week. The Berkshire Athenaeum in Pittsfield, Massachusetts, has convinced many Berkshire County towns to deposit their films in its genealogy and local history department.

Town records on microfilm can be found at various other places. The Massachusetts State Archives has LDS film for many Massachusetts towns (particularly those in the eastern part of the state), and the Maine State Archives, the Connecticut State Library, and the Vermont Public Records Office have copies of most of the films for those states. An ongoing effort called "Adopt-a-Town" encourages people to donate money to the Rhode Island Historical Society for the purchase of microfilmed records of the 39 towns and cities in that state. The collection of town records available on microfilm at the New England Historic Genealogical Society is continually growing.

The researcher should be aware, however, that not everything in the town records may have been filmed. The LDS workers doing the filming, often unacquainted with the jumble and complexity of early New England record-keeping and focusing primarily on vital records, sometimes overlooked other interesting sources such as town council records, tax books, poor records, etc. Also, for the period when town clerks were beginning to keep different types of records in separate volumes, the LDS workers may have filmed only those which obviously contained vital records. At the Maine State Archives, one can find minutes of the town meetings for Wells on microfilm only through the 1770s, the period when they appear in volumes that also contain vital records. After that time, one has to go to the town clerk's office to continue the search of town meetings. Exceptions to this are the towns in Middlesex County, Massachusetts, which were thoroughly covered in a recent demographic study that produced a set of films (non-LDS) which may be found at the Boston Public Library, the Massachusetts Historical Society, and the New England Historic Genealogical

Society. Gloucester, in Essex County, was for some reason included in this set.

A new source for Massachusetts town records exists in the microfiche being produced by Jay Mack Holbrook's Archives Publishing. These microfiche of the original records may be found in the Boston Public Library and other large libraries in New England. Although generally covering only the town vital records, because of the early tendency to mix types of records together, the fiche are worth checking to see what else may be recorded. In Fall River, Massachusetts, for example, one finds mixed in with the vital records the deeds for pews in the Congregational Meetinghouse. For Massachusetts it is also worth checking Carroll C. Wright, *Report on the Custody and Condition of the Public Records of Parishes, Towns, and Counties* (Boston, 1889). Even though this work was compiled more than a hundred years ago, it can be useful to know what records were then in existence.

Once you have located the records of any given town, what can you expect to find there? The first, most obvious, category that comes to mind is the vital records: births, marriages, and deaths. These records have been well covered in other sources and will not be discussed again in this book. The land records that in Rhode Island, Connecticut, and Vermont are found on the town level will not be treated here, nor will the probate records which in Rhode Island are kept by the towns. Instead, we will concentrate on records which relate in some way to the business of the town government, and the various kinds of information they may contain about specific people who lived in the town.

It may be helpful, for the purposes of historical or genealogical research, to think of the different kinds of town records in two categories — although, of course, no such distinction exists in the books themselves. First, there are those records which relate to families who were or became established in the town. These records generally expand our knowledge of such people rather than tell us anything new and different about them. Secondly, there are kinds of records which tell us something about the individuals living in the town who were less prosperous and, because of their poverty or illness, attracted the attention of the town government. Very often the references to these people in the town records provide the only information about them that can be found anywhere, supplying links which may solve long-standing mysteries about family origins.

The researcher must always bear in mind, however, that rigidity of thinking and preconceived notions have no place in genealogical or historical investigation. Exceptions to the rule always exist in any case, and there was inevitably some overlap between the two groups as family fortunes either declined or became more prosperous.

The following pages will cover Freemen and Inhabitancy, Town Officers, Town Business, Land Grants, Boundaries, Treasurer's Records, Tax, Rate, and Assessor's Records, Licenses, Ear or Cattle Marks, Manumissions, Chattel Mortgage Books, Military Records, Poor Records, and Town Reports. There is also a section on Church Records, although in Rhode Island one will not find church matters in town records. Finally there are two sections on inquests and adoptions, although inquests have been found only in the town records of Rhode Island, and adoptions in only one town in Maine.

Chapter Two

Freemen and Inhabitancy

TO THE POLLS, YE SONS OF FREEDOM!

Town Meeting records are most likely to yield information about men who held an established position in the society of the town. These contain, among other things, the lists of freemen and accepted inhabitants. The freemen, freeholders, and recognized male inhabitants were allowed to vote in town meetings, and from their ranks were usually, if not always, drawn the various officers of the town. The qualifications for becoming a freeman or inhabitant or gaining a legal settlement changed over time and from place to place, but generally one had to be male, of a legal age (usually 21, but sometimes as young as 16), own some land in town, and, in some colonies, be a church member. For a more complete discussion of early freeman requirements, see "Legal Qualifications of Voters in Massachusetts," *The Essex Antiquarian*, XII[1908]:145, and Robert Charles Anderson, "The Value of Freemen's Lists," *Great Migration Newsletter*, 1[1990]:17. For the most complete discussion in print of inhabitancy in the six New England states see Josiah Henry Benton, *Warning Out in New England, 1656-1817* (Boston, 1911; reprint, Heritage Books, 1992).

All freemen had to be recognized inhabitants of the town, but not all recognized inhabitants could be freemen. Josiah Benton writes that the inhabitancy laws were

> undoubtedly exercised . . . for the purpose of keeping out persons whose religious or political opinions were unsatisfactory to the towns. But the *reason for the existence* of this right was that inhabitancy, or the right to live in a place, always imposed upon

the inhabitants of the place responsibility for the good conduct
and support of the inhabitant.

The right to live in a town was then understood to imply a right to
have land upon which to live. Therefore, towns admitting new
inhabitants agreed by implication to allot them land from the town
holdings, and to grant them the right to commonage in the town's
common lands. This carried with it the right of free fishing and
fowling in the great ponds and in the rivers and tidal-waters within
the limits of the town.[2]

In Massachusetts the first men to be granted freemanship status
in May 1631 simply asked for the privilege from the Governor and
his Assistants (the ruling body at that time). On 14 May 1634 the
General Court voted itself the power to choose freemen. It further
voted on 3 September 1635 "that none but Freemen shall haue any
vote in any towne, in any accon of aucthoritie, or necessity, or that
which belongs to them by vertue of their Freedome, as receaveing
inhabitants, & layeing out of lots."[3]

Many men were reluctant to become freemen because of the
responsibility in town and colony government that it implied—to
serve as town officers and as jurymen. So on 26 May 1647 the
General Court voted that

> . . . taking into consideration ye usefull ptes & abilities of div^{r}s
> inhabitants amongst us, wch are not freemen . . . it shall & may be
> lawfull for ye freemen . . . to make choyce of such inhabitants,
> though non freemen, who have taken or shall take ye oath of
> fidelity to this goverm^t to be iury men, & to have their vote in y^e
> choyce of ye select men for towne affaires, asseasm^t of rates, and
> other prudentials.

These non-freemen had to be at least 24 years of age and they were not allowed to vote for deputies to the General Court. Later that same year in November it was recognized that many church members had not become freemen, so it was therefore ordered that

> All such memb^rs of churches . . . shall not be exempted from such publike service as they are choose to . . . as cunstables, iurers, selectmen, & survey^rs of high wayes.[4]

In 1658 the General Court repealed the above two laws and decided that "setled inhabitants & house holders" must be 24 years of age, "of honest & good conuersation," rated with £20 of estate, and have taken the oath of fidelity.[5] This remained the basic law until the provincial government of 1692 when freeholders and other inhabitants who were rated at £20 were given the right to vote for town officers. The term *freeman* was no longer used in Massachusetts after this time. Since Maine was part of Massachusetts until 1820, its inhabitancy laws are the same.

Benton comments, "In no part of New England was the admission of inhabitants, transfer of land, and warning out of persons who sought to be inhabitants without being admitted by the towns more carefully guarded than in Connecticut." The qualifications for inhabitants as of 26 February 1656 were "housholders that are one & twenty yeares of age, or haue bore office, or haue £30 estate." In 1660 the General Court ordered that no one could be accepted as an inhabitant who was not known to be of "an honest conversation" and had not been accepted by vote by a majority of a town's current inhabitants. It was also ordered that no one could sell his house or land unless the town's inhabitants voted to allow the sale. As late as 1888 one still had to become an inhabitant "by vote of the inhabitants of the town or consent of the civil authority and selectmen without such vote, or by being appointed to and executing some public office."[6]

In Lebanon, Connecticut, on 19 December 1706 "At a Leagall Town meeting of y[e] inhabitants of Lebanon . . . thay then axepted of Richard Man . . . John Loomis . . . Nathall Bingham Stephen Tilden and Benjamin Phelps to be inhabitants in the place."[7]

The term *freeman* continues in use to this day in Vermont and Rhode Island. An Act passed in Vermont in 1797 defining a legal settlement included

> . . . every person who shall purchase a freehold estate of the value
> of one hundred dollars . . . and shall actually occupy and improve
> the same for the term of one whole year; or shall actually . . .
> have rented and occupied a tenement of the yearly value of
> twenty dollars or upwards, for the term of two whole years . . . ;
> and every person who shall . . . have executed any public office or
> charge in such town or place, during one whole year, or shall
> have been charged with and paid his or her share of the public
> rates or taxes of such town or place for the space of two years;
> and every person who shall have been bound as apprentice . . .
> have served a term not less than three years next preceding the
> time of such apprentice's arriving at the age of twenty-one years,
> if a male, or . . . eighteen years, if a female . . . shall be deemed . . .
> to have attained a legal settlement . . . ; and every other healthy
> able bodied person coming and residing within this state, and
> being of peaceable behaviour, shall be deemed . . . to be legally
> settled in the town or place in which he or she shall have first
> resided for the space of one whole year; and every bastard child
> shall be deemed . . . to be settled in the town or place of the last
> legal settlement of his or her mother. [8]

To vote in town meetings in Vermont, one still today must take the Freeman's Oath administered by a public official.

The same qualifications of gender, age, and ownership of property were applied to freemen in Rhode Island, but never was church membership a consideration there. On 13 May 1638 in Portsmouth it was "Ordered, that none shall be received as inhabitants or Freemen, to build or plant upon the Island but such as shall be received in by the consent of the Bodye, and do submitt to the Government."[9]

In 1718, New Hampshire passed an Act that said that

> . . . no person whatever coming to reside or dwell in any town in this province, other than freeholders and proprietors of land in such town, or those born, or that have served as apprenticeship there . . . shall be admitted to the privilege of elections in such towns."[10]

Occasionally a man would petition to become an inhabitant of a town, as did Daniel Gideons in 1796:[11]

> At a Legal Town Meeting holden at Claremont [New Hampshire] on Tuesday 8th Day of March 1796 Daniel Gideons presented a Petition requesting to be received as a free holder and an Inhabitant of said Claremont . . . Voted to grant the request of said Petition.

Other men who did not own enough property to fit the qualification, and even women and children, could be recognized inhabitants of a town or gain a legal settlement, thus becoming eligible to receive support and services from the town if necessary. The condition of being a recognized inhabitant of a town was synonymous with having a legal settlement there. For more information on the importance of inhabitancy or having a settlement, see the chapter on Poor Records.

In some places the eldest son of a freeman might be granted that status when he reached the age of 21, even though he owned no land—probably on the assumption that he would eventually inherit his father's property. Occasionally you will find someone listed as a freeman before he reached 21, and these cases usually, upon study, tell you something about the individual that may not be otherwise apparent. His father may have died, or he may have recently married and set up farming on his own, or perhaps he was especially able in some way which made the town want his participation even though he was under age. In 1762, the Rhode Island General Assembly, concerned that the towns were accepting too many new freemen, directed the town clerks to make lists explaining the qualifications of each man given that status since 1760. The resulting lists, at the Rhode Island Archives and transcribed in *Rhode Island Roots*, provide a considerable amount of genealogically and biographically useful information.[12]

Chapter Three

Town Officers

The freemen and inhabitants of each town met at specified intervals in town meetings, and careful records were kept of the business transacted at these sessions. At least one town meeting was held each year, usually in March or April, at which the officials for the coming year were elected. From the records of these meetings one can glean various information about the men concerned and their positions in the social structure of the town. For example, on 2 March 1719 in Reading, Massachusetts, a General Town Meeting held "by the freeholders and other inhabitants of said town qualifide as the law directs, regularly assembled," chose as their moderator Capt. Jonathan Pool.[13]

Francis Smith was chosen *town clerk*, his legible recording of the minutes attesting to his aptitude for the job. Massachusetts adopted the *Body of Liberties* in 1641 and *The Laws and Liberties of Massachusetts* in 1648. Both of these documents made it a duty for the town to keep records of births, marriages, and deaths and the land owned by each inhabitant. In 1650 Connecticut established a "Code of Laws" in which the "Town Clarke or Register" was to "record all Births and Deaths of persons in theire Towne . . . allso that every new married man shall likewise bring in a certificate of his Marriage . . . to the said Register . . . Allso . . . record euery mans howse and lands. . . ."[14] In the records of the individual towns the clerks were further ordered, as in the case of Watertown in 1634, to "keep the Records and Acts of the Towne."[15] And likewise when Vermont set down its laws in 1779 the town clerks were to "record all marriages, births, and deaths . . . record every man's house and lands . . . And . . . enter . . . all votes of the said town, grants, or conveyances of lands, choice of town officers, and other town acts. . . ."[16]

Five *selectmen*, including Francis Smith, were chosen by Reading "to order and manige the prudenthal affaires of yᵉ town for the insueing year;" Francis Smith recorded them as Mr. Thomas Bancroft, Esq. John Goodwin, Lt. William Bryant, and Mr. Benjamin Harnden, but he did not add any prefix to his own name. One may safely assume that the chosen men were of known ability and position in the community. Until the 1690s the term *townsman* was used in Connecticut instead of *selectman*, and in Rhode Island men chosen for this function were called *town councilors*.

The selectmen, town councilors, or townsmen were designated to act for the town in most matters and they "functioned as all-around political handymen."[17] In the early years of a town these men often performed all the duties that would later be done by moderators, treasurers, assessors, tithingmen, and other officers. At a town meeting in 1659, New London, Connecticut, provided its townsmen with a list of the twelve duties expected of them. It is interesting to compare this list with the forty-one duties listed for selectmen in Massachusetts by 1793 (see Appendix B). The New London townsmen were to:

1. "Keep up" town bounds and supervise the fence viewers.
2. See that children are educated and servants well ordered, and that there is no living in idleness.
3. Maintain town and colony laws and provide the town magazine with arms and ammunition.
4. Maintain the streets, lanes, highways, and common lands

and provide some method of calling forth individuals to work on them.

5. Take care of the meetinghouse.
6. "Consider of some absolute and perfect way and course to be taken for a perfect platform of settling and maintaining of records respecting the towns, that they be fully clearly and fairly kept, for the use, benefit and peaceful state of the town and after posterity."
7. Control the agenda of town meetings and prevent needless discussion.
8. Regulate matters concerning Indians.
9. Regulate the felling, sawing, and transportation of all timber, boards, masts, and pipestaves.
10. Oversee the ferries.
11. Determine all complaints regarding land grants except "difficult" cases that were to be referred to the meeting.
12. Hold regular meetings of their own and give an advance notice of their times and locations.[18]

The next officers chosen in Reading were two *constables*, Timothy Goodwin "for the town" and John Upton Jr. "for the North Precent." This tells us that Goodwin lived in town and Upton in the part set off as the North Precinct, a geographical fact which may prove useful. Constables were often the very first officials chosen when a new town was formed; they were the "policemen" of colonial New England. In Connecticut the constable was the first town office created by the General Court in 1636 and by 1658 in Massachusetts this position had twenty-six duties.[19]

Reading March y͏ͤ 2ᵈ 1719 when a Generall Town meeting held By the freeholders and other Inhabitants of s͏ͩ Town qualifiede as the Law Directs Regularly assembled

Cap͏ͭ Jonathan Poole was Chosen Moderator

Select men accompt of the Town Debts alowed

Francis Smith was Chosen Town Clerk

Francis Smith
M͏ͬ Thomas Bancrofe   } was Chosen Select men to order and
E͏ͩ John Goodwin   } Manige the Prudenthal affaires of y͏ͤ Town
L͏ͭ William Bryant &   } for That Insueing year
M͏ͬ Benjamin Harnden   }

There was Chosen for Constables Timothy Goodwin for the Town and John Vpton Jun͏ͭ for the North Precenct

Thomas Daman
M͏ͬ Peter Emerson
Benjamin Burnap
Joseph Rist   } was Chosen
John Townsend   } Tithing men
Thomas Tayler
& John Phelps

E͏ͩ John Wesson
Samuel Daman
John Bacheler   } was Chosen
Nathanel Parker Ju͏ͬ } Surveyers
Ezekel Vpton Ser   } of High
& Adam Hart   } Ways

Ebenezer Emerson
Joseph Daman   } was Chosen
Isaac Smith   } Fence
John Fish   } Viewers
William Sawyer
& Ebenezer Flint

Jeremiah Swayn
James Smith
Samuel Lillie Jun͏ͬ   } was Chosen
Henry Sawyer   } Swine offic͏ͤ
Joseph Vpton Jun͏ͬ
& Ebenezer Fish

E͏ͩ John Goodwin was Chosen Sealer of wayts and meas͏ͬ

Benjamin Hartshorn was Chosen Sealer of Leather

M͏ͬ Thomas Nickols was Chosen Grand Juryman for the year

After the constables, there follow the names of seven men chosen in Reading to be *tithingmen*. Their duties were, first, to see to it that everyone in town made their proper contributions to the meetinghouse and the minister's salary and, second, to ensure church attendance of all inhabitants. Although church and state were theoretically separate in New England, the fact that most early towns elected tithingmen illustrates that in reality the two were very close together; each town was built around the church — usually called a meetinghouse — at its center, and the minister must be paid. In the records of Rhode Island, on the other hand, where state and church really were separate and religious freedom was a carefully guarded right, one never finds tithingmen.

More town voters are named as the list of Reading's officers continues. Ebenezer Emerson, Joseph Daman, Isaac Smith, John Fish, William Sawyer, and Ebenezer Flint were chosen *fence viewers*. As the New England poet Robert Frost knew, "good fences make good neighbors" — it was important that the fences and stone walls which marked the boundaries of a man's property with his next-door neighbors be correctly placed and kept in good repair, lest his animals get out and damage someone else's land. If a man neglected his fences, he would be fined; disputes often escalated out of the town records and into the courts fairly rapidly when sheep or cows got onto someone else's land and ate whatever they found there.

In Reading, in 1719, John Weston, Samuel Daman, John Bacheler, Nathaniel Parker Jr., Ezekiel Upton Sr., and Adam Hart were chosen *surveyors of highways*. Their job was to see that all the roads in town were in good repair and located where they were supposed to be, and to determine when the paths that went from house to house and from town to town were used enough to warrant becoming roads. The creation of roads usually involved taking land from someone, so it is not unusual to find in a town record that a man was given a piece of land elsewhere in town to compensate for some he had lost to a new road or the moving of an old one. People sometimes traded land in order that new roads could be more conveniently located. In Rhode Island, towns were divided into districts, sometimes called squadrons; each landholder was responsible for maintaining the roads in his district a certain number of days during the year. These highway lists help in determining just where a certain ancestor lived in relation to his neighbors.

On 16 May 1806 the selectmen of Northwood, New Hampshire, notified Solomon Buzel, Esq., one of the surveyors of highways, that

> . . . you are Requirad to see that Every person having his name set Down here in said List works out propotion on the highway here set Down in the said List at the Rate of six Cents per hour for hand Labor and the same for oxen wheals and plow. You are to Repair the Highway from Notingham Line to Doctor Wiere from their to Barington Line. any person Refusing to work out His propotion set Down here in said List you are to Distrain for the same as the Law Directs and make Return of this warrant with your Doings therein by the first of June 1807.

This was followed by a list of men with amounts in dollars and cents after their names representing their work.[20]

Returning to Reading as our example, we find that five men were chosen in 1719 as *swine officers*; in some other places they might be called *hog reeves*. Whatever the title, the job was to oversee the care of all the pigs and cattle in town. There has been speculation that men chosen as hog reeves were that year's bridegrooms, but although in many cases these men had indeed been married within the year, that was probably not the reason for their being chosen. Hog reeve was an entry level position in town government. Therefore, a man who was newly married would also be likely to begin his service to the town at roughly the same time. Of the nine men in the first three generations of the Bryant family in Reading, only one was elected to this position within a year after his marriage. Four were elected within two years after marriage, two were elected more than two years but less than five years after marriage, and two were elected before they were married.[21]

Some jobs simply had to be filled year after year, and the choice of any particular man might mean only that he was willing to take on the obligation. On the other hand, the appointment of the same man year after year to the same position may indicate something about his particular occupation or aptitude. The job of the man who was chosen *sealer of weights and measures* was to check all measures used for the sale of various goods in town, a function which still exists today, although not on the town level. In Reading, in 1719, Benjamin Hartshorn was chosen *sealer of leather*, suggesting that he may have been a cordwainer or tanner, both tradesmen who worked regularly with leather. It would be his task to inspect the tanned skins needed in those times not only for shoes but for saddles, bridles, and many other items used about the farm and household.

Other men were chosen to mind cattle, see to the yoking of oxen, and whatever tasks were considered important to the welfare of the town and its people. Some town offices are unique to a particular town or region because of the resources or occupations of that area: Hatfield, Massachusetts, chose a "Gauger & Surveyor of Casks" or "Gauger of Tar & Pine Casks," Pepperell chose "Informers about Deers" (later called deer reeves), Medford chose "Wood Corders," "Salt Measurers," and "Bread Weighers."

The size of a particular town might also have determined the number and variety of town offices. The example used above for Reading shows that town chose one town clerk, four selectmen, two constables, seven tithingmen, six surveyors of highways, six fence viewers, five swine officers, and one sealer of leather. By contrast Ipswich, Massachusetts, in 1720/1 (just a year later than the Reading example) chose one town clerk, seven selectmen, four constables, twelve tithingmen, one town treasurer, one overseer of the poor, twenty surveyors of highways, six haywards, one town cryer, one pound keeper, fifteen fence viewers, seven corders of wood, seventeen hog reeves, four cullers of fish, two gaugers of casks, two sealers of leather, and two clerks of the market.[22] For more complete information on the duties and responsibilities of each town office, see Appendix B, which abstracts a book on the subject published in Boston in 1793.[23]

Besides serving as chosen town officers, men were expected also to serve on various committees appointed as needed by the town. These might include managing such tasks as finding a new minister, laying out a new highway, preparing deeds when the town laid out new lots, or settling boundary disputes between neighbors or neighboring towns.

Researching town records for anyone who was a landowner in colonial times is almost certain to turn up a man's public service career through a succession of jobs and committee assignments, for every inhabitant was expected to fulfill his obligations as a citizen.

If for some reason he could not, the fact and the reason are often mentioned; if he refused to serve, he could be fined. Election as a selectman or town councilman was the top of the ladder, and many men served in that capacity for years.

Appointments as *jurors* or deputies to the General Court or Assembly, as the case might be, were also recorded in the town meeting records. To qualify as a juror a man had to own some property. On 24 December 1782, in Unity, New Hampshire, the town was to choose "two Good and Lawfull men having an Estate or freehold worth forty Shillings per Annum or a personal Estate of the value of fifty Pounds Stearling one to Searve on the Petit Jury at the next Inferiorer Court of Common pleas . . . one to Serve on the Petit Jury at the next Court of General sesions."[24] Deputies were chosen from the town's leading men.

Chapter Four

Town Business

Τ he town could and would deal with almost any matter that affected it in any way. In Massachusetts:

> In spite of a regard for uniformity in general matters, the General Court placed few restrictions on the local legislative powers of the towns. Local communities could, of course, pass no ordinances incompatible with the regulations of the colony. They were restricted, also, in the amount of fines to be imposed, the method of disposing of their lands, and the duties and choice of minor officials.[25]

The following examples show the wide variety of matters that might confront the town fathers.

The third record book of Simsbury, Connecticut, begins by noting that the "Sims Bery Town Book of Record" was "Received of Saml Humphris johns Son August the fifth 1719 price -0-10-0."[26]

About 1650 Roxbury, Massachusetts, voted that "two hookes should be provided for pulling down of houses (in case of fire) at the town charge."[27]

At a town meeting on 1 March 1670/1 at Hull, Massachusetts, the selectmen listed many laws and the fines for not complying with them.[28] Most of these regulations dealt with the building and maintaining of fences or stone walls, which were to be 3 feet 10 inches high and 10 inches broad by April 20 or the owner faced a fine of 2^s/6^d; every person was to set up a stake marked with the first two letters of his name at the ends of the fences or pay a fine of 12^d; animals must be kept contained at night and not let into the sown fields, etc. At the same meeting, it was directed that "whoever be found smocking of tobaco in any barn or other place wher any straw or cumbustabell stufe is for dangor of fire upon the penelty of 12ˢ a tim half to the town and half to the informer."

Using town records can sometimes be frustrating because the record keepers did not always fully explain what was happening. On 1 October 1688 the selectmen of Woburn, Massachusetts, "agreed that Mathew Johnson Senʳ and James Convers second should goe (forthwith) to Wᵐ Johnson Esqʳ and demand the Towne books of him that are not yett delivered." They went to William Johnson, but reported that he "refused to deliver the Town books to the Townsmen order." It is never explained why Johnson would not return the books, nor could a record be found in the town meetings that he ever did so.[29]

On 18 September 1699 the Selectmen of Woburn were

> Informed that Jacob Hamblet was so outragously distracted, and tore all his Cloaths off his back from time to time nothing would hold him, and that his wife was no longer able to subsist without som help from the towne, they ordered Jamˢ Berbeen Constable to make a suit of Sailcloth (upon yᵉ Towns accᵗ) and to sew it strong, and make it to lace behind, yᵗ so he may not be able to get yᵗ off.[30]

Ipswich, Massachusetts, voted,

> Affirmatively That if any p[e]rson or p[e]rsons from This Town shall suffer any Dog Little or great to Come Into the Meeting house on yᵉ Sabbath or Lectur Days The Ownʳ of such Dogs being Convicted yʳ of before any Justice of the peace shall pay yᵉ sum of one shilling one halfe yʳ of To the Complaineʳ & yᵉ other halfe to yᵉ overseers of yᵉ poor for yᵉ Use of yᵉ poor for Every such Conviction.[31]

New Haven, Connecticut, voted on 27 December 1708,

In Consideration of the great Damage done by black birds yearly
. . . do order that every male person a bove the age of sixteen
years to the age of Seventy years (except the minister) Shall Kill
or destroy one dozen of black birds . . . for what number more
then one Dozen any person or persons Shall Kill or destroy he or
they Shall be paid one peny for each bird . . . and if any person . . .
Shall not Kill or destroy one Dozen of said birds he or they Shall
pay into the town Treasurer one Shilling or one peny for each
bird that he Shall fall Short of a Dozen.[32]

In Cape Elizabeth, Maine, on 26 October 1778, the selectmen
received the report of a committee that advised:[33]

That there be a vote passed that if any person shall pass by or
within Forty Rods of the House where Josiah Sawyer & his
family now is in Sick with the Small Pox, until said family and
house is cleansed except they first obtain leave of the Selectmen
. . . the Doctor & nurse only excepted, under the penalty of Fifty
pound . . . & that any person or persons that now is or shall Go
into the Hospital at Falmouth for Innoculation shall not come
into this Town under the Term of Thirty five Days . . . & that no
person shall go from this Town nearer than Fifty Rods to said
Hospital to carry Provisions to the sick and said Persons shall not
come nearer to any . . . person that shall come out of said
Hospital to Receive said Provisions than Twenty Rods under the
Penalty of Fifty pounds.

On 26 December 1726, New Haven, Connecticut, voted that

. . . [since] the Boys playing in the market place is mischievous for
by that means the meeting house windows are often shamfully
Broken, for the preventing whereof it is Resolved . . . that for the
future the Boys shall not be allowed to play in the market place
within 20 Rod of the meeting house on the penalty of 12 pence
for Every such offence.[34]

In Simsbury, Connecticut, on 28 December 1732 it was voted,

. . . that twelve bulls be hired at the towns Cost and for the Towns Use for five years next Coming and that the hire of them shall be as followeth twenty shillings a year to be paid to the person or persons that shall procure a good three year old bull for the Towns use and fifteen shillings to the person or persons that shall procure a good two year old bull for the towns use.[35]

The towns of Northampton, Hadley, Hatfield, and Deerfield, Massachusetts, were looking for a doctor to settle and serve these towns, so on 17 March 1739 it was voted in Deerfield,

. . . that M[r] John Catlin be appointed to go to Hatfield and Meet the Com[ttees] of Northampton Hadley & Hatfield and there in y[e] behalf of this town to act and determine what to give Doct[r] Forter for his Encouragement to Settle as a bone Setter in this part of y[e] County that is to Say whether to give Fourteen Pounds or what part Soever thereof Shall be by him accounted to be our proportion with y[e] rest of the towns Considering y[e] Circumstances of y[e] town with regard to their distance from him.[36]

On 21 March 1776, Unity, New Hampshire, agreed and voted[37]

. . . that all ox Slads for the futere In this Town Shall be four feet wide from Inside to Inside of the Runers in order to Brake open the Snow in the Highways to accommodate our Selves and the Neighbouring Towns for Transporting and the Roads be kept open in the winter seson and Eveary man in the Town according to his proportion turn out after the falling of a Snow in order to make paths in the publick Roads to Each Town Line.

When Granby, Connecticut, was set off from Simsbury in 1786, one of the first votes of the new town was to set up a committee to

. . . assist the Select Men in Setling accounts with the Town of Simsbury in Dividing the Town Stock & Town Debts & Town poor and other Buisness Consurning the Devision of the Town the Present year.[38]

On 4 March 1799 New Braintree, Massachusetts, voted in

> Respect to fencing the Burying yards . . . That the Town will
> fence one in a year . . . the present year to fence the one by the
> Meeting House, the second the one by Capt Warrins, the Third
> on the Plain, and the Fourth that by Mr Nathan Thomsons.[39]

Chittenden, Vermont, voted in 1804

> . . . to pay their proportion of a premium of 10 Dollars for each
> grown wolf after the first Day of May and previous to the first
> Day of January next, taken killed and Destroyed within the
> towns of Philadelphia Pittsford Rutland Brandon or Chittenden.[40]

A man might even ask the town clerk to register certain items in the town books to make sure that they were made part of the official record. This probably explains the following entry in the Deerfield, Massachusetts, book:[41]

> Having received Power from Congress to discharge I do hereby
> discharge Neverson Warren Soldier in the 3d Massachusetts Regt
> from any further Service in said Corps he having served the term
> of three years —
> Given under my hand and seal at Pecks kill this 24th Day of
> December 1779   J. Greaton Colo[nel]

> A true Copy test Justin Hitchcock Town Clerk.

Or these two entries from Marlborough, Connecticut:[42]

> August Term 1835 . . . I hereby Certify that Oliver Colemane . . .
> was Convicted of theft before the County Court . . . And
> Sentenced to imprisonment for Sixty days in the County Goal &
> a fine of twenty dollars. . . .

> Certificate of Manufacturing Stock
>   I hereby certify that the Capital stock of the Marlborough
> Manufacturing Company is forty two thousand Dollars . . . 26th
> June 1818.

Chapter Five

Land Grants

Another type of record that can help to fill out the picture of a property-owning ancestor is the land grant. It is not unusual to find record of an ancestor selling land for which there is no purchase deed in evidence. He may, of course, have inherited it and there are known cases of unrecorded deeds, but if nothing can be found to indicate that such was the case, chances are that the land was a grant from the town. At the time when most towns were established, they held a specified amount of land by grant from the colony or state legislature. The original inhabitants were all given town lots (or house lots) and field lots, often made up of specified upland, swamp, meadowland, and land in common, and they also had rights in future divisions of land as the town became more developed. Such rights were frequently sold, with deeds containing reference to rights in land "divided and undivided." Usually the only condition attached to these grants was that the new owner might not sell the land to a non-inhabitant without permission of the town fathers, but one example has been found of a more restrictive condition: On 24 December 1686 Simsbury, Connecticut, granted a house lot to James Miles for five years, directing him to "make Emprovment of Said land by fenceing Buildg Breaking up at ye s^d land Before he shall have any power to Alienate s^d land."[43]

In the 1660s, Barnstable, Plymouth Colony (now Massachusetts), recorded the land owned by each man.[44] "The Lands of ye Heirs of Henry Coggin" were listed as follows:

1. A house lott of Upland Containing Eight acres . . .
   bounded Easterly by yᵉ pond Westerly by yʳ own
   Marsh Northerly by their own . . . Southerly partly
   by their own Land and partly by yᵉ Land in possession
   of John Binney.
2. Four acres of Marsh . . . adjoining by yᵉ Upland bounded
   Easterly & Northerly by Henry Bourns Marsh.
3. Four acres Upon Jewells Island.
4. Eight acres of Marsh . . . bounded Northerly Upon yᵉ
   Upland Southerly Upon yᵉ Creek, Easterly by Isaac
   Wells, Westerly by Henry Bourn.
5. One acre of Upland adjoining thereto.
6. Fifty acres of Upland butting Easterly upon yᵉ Indian
   Pond Westerly Into Commons Northerly by Isaac Wells
   Southerly by Henry Bourn.
7. One acre and half of Upland . . . adjoining to sᵈ Home
   Lot bounded Easterly by yᵉ pond Westerly by yᵉ Land in
   possession of John Phinney Southerly by yᵉ High Way.
8. One Acre . . . of Upland adjoining to yᵉ sᵈ home lott
   bounded Westerly by Henry Bourn Easterly by yᵉ sᵈ
   John Phinney Southerly by yᵉ High way.
9. Two shares in yᵉ Calves Pasture about an acre . . .
   bounded Easterly by James Hamblin Westerly by John
   Phinney.

"A List of the mens Names that have Drawn there lots and of
the Sechedull 1749" for Chichester, New Hampshire, begins with
the following six names:[45]

> Nattˡˡ Gookin the 6 Range No 23
> John Odlin the 6 Range No 25
> Chrisʳ Page the 8 Range No 3
> Petter Weare Junʳ the 26 lote in yᵉ 5 Range
> Edward West the 21 lote in the 2 Range
> Nattˡˡ Healy 5 Range No 12

90

A Plan of Forty Eight acres of Land
Laid out to Satisfie Mrs Hannah
Beamons Draught or Lot Number
Eighty one in the Land North of
Cheepside and East of Green River &
whichd Land Lyeth on the West
Side of the Road that Goeth from ye
falls to Northfield and Joyns to it
and is bounded and Deliniated as
in the plan Surveyd July the
24: 1736

ℓ Elijah Williams Surveyr

Accepted pr
Elijah Williams
Thᵒ Wells
Samˡˡ Childs
} Comtⁱ

A plot of thirty one acres & ... Rods of
Land Laid out to Samuel Bardwell
to Satisfie his Draught or Lot Noo
... of Land East of Green River &c
which Land Lyeth in ye Swampey
or Low Lands ... Hill Against ... Hill
Of all ... Callid beginning at a stake
& Stone ...

No 35 Eˡ 6 perches

93

A plat of Sixty three acres and Sixty six
rods of Land Laid out to Jonathan Wells
Esqr to Satisfie his Draught or Lot 124,
Eighty Seven In the Land East of Green river
be which Land lyeth on ye Mill Brook
So Called as Described in ye plan & on
ye road west, on John Arms plat & South
boundes and Deliniated as in the
plan Surveyed July 31st 1736 and
protracted p Elijah Williams Survey

Elijah Williams
John Catlin   Comtee
Thos Wells

A plat of Land containing
Eighty Acres Laid out to ye heirs
of Mehuman Hinsdell Deceasd to
Satesfie his Draught in ye Land
East of Green River &c No 88 which
Land Lyeth joyning on a plat of
Jonᵗ Wells Esqr South & on a plat of
ye Heirs No 76 which plat butteth
on a highway Lying between
Green river & Mill Brook So Called
& is bounded & Delineated as
in ye plan Survey Aug 13th 1736
& protracted p Elijah Williams Survey

Thomas French
Elijah Williams

In Newport, Rhode Island, small town lots were set aside for tradesmen and in 1712 in Hatfield, Massachusetts, it was voted by the town:[46]

> That whereas Jeremiah Waite and Jos. Waite mooved to the
> Town for the use of the land in Hatfield adjacent to the Great
> Pond, on the West side, and between the Meadow fence, and said
> Pond, on condition that they . . . do maintain from year to year
> the meadow fence sufficiently and secure the Great Meadow from
> any damage by creatures coming through said Pond, into said
> Meadow . . . until the Proprietors shall forbid the same.

In Bernardston, Massachusetts, on 3 December 1781, it was

> voted that Stephen Webster shall have Liberty to improve the
> land laid out for a burying yard in town Except where the corps
> are buryed, for the term of 10 years in consideration of his
> clearing said land & fencing it with chestnut rails which he is to
> git on the Ministry lot.[47]

In the very early 18th century in Natick, Massachusetts, there is a series of Indian deeds written in the Indian language developed by John Eliot.[48]

In 1728 Richard Shatchwell told the Ipswich, Massachusetts, selectmen that he "moved to the Town that he might have Some Consideration to be laid out on his Grandfather Richd Shatchwell decd his Land at a place leading to Green Points Creek So Called Anno 1667 for which he Says there has been no Satisfaction made." A committee was appointed "to hear the Motion" and "report as soon as conveniently may be what be proper to be done thereon."[49]

As a town grew and the need for new roads developed, land was often taken from residents, who were then reimbursed with property elsewhere, as shown by these two examples from Unity, New Hamsphire:[50]

I Benjamin Clough of Unity have Received of the Selectmen of
Unity Six Rods of Range way Begining near William Perkins
House thence Runing two Rods west of my old House to a Stake
and Stones Infull Satisfaction for the Roade going through my
land South of my New House and So to the Range by Perkins
House. . . . Unity September 18th 1797.

I Jesse Hill of Unity have Received of the Selectmen of Unity two
Rods of the Range way at the south end of the lot of land, No
Eliven in the Second Range in full Compensation for the Roade
Going through my Land. Unity June 19th 1797.

Along with deeds for the lands granted by the town, or lists of
the lots received in later divisions, the town records may contain
maps of lot layouts. In Sherborn, Massachusetts, there is a
collection of maps from the early 1700s showing sections of the
town. Included on these maps are the names of the owners of the
lots, the amount of acreage in each lot, names of the men whose
land bounded the lots, natural features such as roads, creeks, and
rivers, town boundary lines, and markers such as stakes and stones
and trees. Many have little trees drawn on the maps with the
notations of "White oak" or "Black oake." [51]

"Records of the Pocomtuck Proprietors, 1699-1799" of
Deerfield, Massachusetts, includes maps and descriptions of the lots
laid out to each man. There is also a list that includes the lot
numbers, the name of the person who drew each lot, the name of
the person in whose right the lot was drawn (if different), the
number of acres and rods in each lot, and the associated amount of
right in common land which might be divided later. Many of the
people were drawing lots in their own rights, but most were
drawing on the rights of others. Those that have the same surname
(Ebenezer Hinsdell on the right of Mehuman Hinsdell, Stephen

Williams on the right of Mr. John Williams, Sarah Smead on the right of Samuel Smead deceased) obviously suggest a close relationship between the two people, while those with different surnames (Aaron Denvir on the right of Hannah Beaman, Thomas Bardwell on the right of Ebenezer Brooks, Jacob Warner on the right of Hannah Beaman) may not indicate a relationship, but still present a possibility that is worth researching.

The tax records will often include lists of non-resident land owners. If these non-residents failed to keep up with their taxes, the town might sell the land, as happened in Croyden, New Hampshire in 1814:[52]

> Dr. Torry's Land original Proprietor Wm. Dudley Lot No 52 a 60 Acre Lot, Taxes & Cost 25 Acres of said Lot bid off by James Powers, at the west End & paid by him . . . $207.

> Nathl Hall's Land, original Proprietor Timothy Darling Lot No 32 a 60 acre Lot Taxes & Cost The whole . . . bid off by John Allen Jr [for] $207.

Chapter Six

Boundary and Border Disputes

own records may include accounts of boundary disputes between neighboring communities. These may sometimes refer back to decisions made many years earlier, as in this example from New Haven, Connecticut in 1701:[53]

Whereas by an instrument bearing Date the fifth Day of october in year 1669 there is a setling of the Line betwene the towns of new haven and branford as is more fully therein exsprest which Instrument is upon Record and afterward upon somm after Considerations the said townes of Branford and new haven made another and new Line for som part of the bounds as may more fully appear in a Deed bearing Date the eight Day of may in the year of our Lord 1682 in which Deed for Reasons and Conditions therin exsprest the said towne of branford did Release or alow to new haven towne half an mile out of the former stated bounds and so the Line betwene the two townes to be half a mile eastwardly of what it was before for the full issue and settlement of which Line moses mansfield, abraham Dickerman Deputed by the towne of new haven and took with them John potter, sam'll hemenway, and enos Talmadge survayor and from branford samuell pond and John frisbee Deputeed by their Towne upon the thirtieth Day of november [1685] meet at the head of the great pond from which pond northward is the alteration which is before exsprest from the head of which pond half a mile eastwardly is the first station wher there is a whit oake tree marked with H and TB with a heap of stones case at the Roote and from that station a straight Line Runing north bearing eastward of the top of the hill which hill is eastward of a boggy meadow out of which Runeth a brook called hercules Brook the said station is a whit oak tree marked with som Letters or marks

and many stones Laid at the Roote of it and from the said state on
the top of the hill the Line to be a north line with the Just
variation according to the contry to the end of their Bounds.

The town records of Natick, Massachusetts, show that on 5 July
1784 John Jones and Adams Jones from Dedham and Hezekiah
Broad and Ephraim Dana from Natick were "legally authorized to
Perambulate . . . the Boundaries on the lines between the Towns of
Dedham and Natick." The bounds were described by the people on
whose land the boundary lay, including John Jones, William Bacon
Jr., David Cleaveland, John Battle, Jeremiah Bacon, Timothy
Allen, heirs of Thomas Ellis, Ebenezer Battle, and John Ephraim.[54]
Many New England towns still perambulate or walk the
boundaries every year, and Boston perambulates the ward
boundaries.

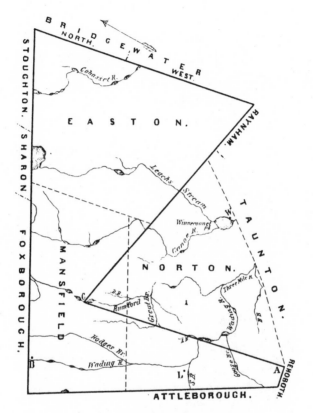

MAP
OF
TAUNTON NORTH PURCHASE
AND THE TOWNS OF
NORTON, EASTON AND MANSFIELD.
———×———

EXPLANATIONS

———— *Bounds of North Purchase.*

- - - - - *Bounds of Towns.*

↥ *Cong. Parish Church of Norton.*

JH Buffords Lith Boston.   Scale 2½ miles to an inch

49

Chapter Seven

Treasurer's Records

own treasurer's accounts also provide interesting information about the lives of our ancestors. Some treasurers simply listed people's names and the amounts paid to them, but fortunately most treasurers included some reason why the payments were made. The variety of payments made by the treasurer of Billerica, Massachusetts, on 29 September 1790 offers a good example of the wide range of concerns of the town:[55]

> To Jon^a Bowen treasurar for a abatement of sundry poor persons taxes in Liut. Farmer's town Rates for 1786.

> To Jesse French for a Door Stone to the Meeting house which his Father found many years ago.

> To Thos Goodwin for 1½ bushells of Indian meal for the widow Danforth.

> To Saml Bowen for paying Nabby griffin for keeping the School 4½ weeks.

> To Sears Cook for renewing Wilmington line.

> To John Beard for making a fram for the meeting house Bell.

> To Dr Francis Kittredge for visits and medicines for Tim° Toothaker.

> To Joseph Shed for boarding Ruth Dow, 1 week.

> To Edward Farmer Esqr for sundry Days attending the Courts Committe and attending the Court.

> To him for his service as an assessor Seven Days and a half. To him for Cash p^d to Mr. Sullivan in the Contest with Chelmsford.

To him for a journey to Groton.

To Eph^m Crosby for boarding Abigail Kidder 13 weeks including some nursing.

To Jon^a Bowen treasurer for paying Mr Cogin for preaching 6 Sabbaths.

To John Dike for Lime Rum and Sugar expended at the meeting house.

To Jesse Simonds for mending shoes for David Kemp.

To Benj^a Needham for 25½ feet of wood for the widow Danforth.

To him for keeping a Cow for her.

To Jon^a Bowen treasurer for paying sundry due Bills being for timber and Labour at the meeting house.

To Josiah Crosby for 4 y^d of woolen Cloth for Tim° Toothaker.

Treasurer records are the best place in which to find information on the town's poor people in the eighteenth century. The Treasurer's book for Lincoln, Massachusetts, from 1755 to 1788 contains several different kinds of information on the poor, or those who had fallen on hard times.[56] Thirty different people or families were listed by name as being warned out of town.

The town of Lincoln paid many of its residents for supplies or services they rendered to the poor. Examples include ". . . for subsisting the widow Conant," "bording the wife of Saml Whiteker," "shoos for Tabitha Whitacer," ". . . for meat [pork] Delivered to the widow Mary Gage," "for visits and medicines for Pegg Arpin," "five loads of wood for the wife of Daniel Hager . . . for supporting his father and mother," "for weaving twenty two yeards of Cloth for Mary Oliver . . . for making two shifts a short gown & petty coat & two aprons," and "for boarding Huldah Whitaker twelve weeks and for Apothecary's Drugs and Wine which he purchased for her and his Horse for her to go to the Doctor."

The town also arranged for some of the children of the poor to become apprentices: "for taking Tabitha Whitaker as an apprentis until she is eighteen," "having taken Huldah Whitacer by an indenture till she is eighteen," "according to the agreement the selectmen made with him to incourage him to take the widow Elizabeth Billings youngest Child named Betty & to keep it till it shall arrive to the age of Eighteen," and "for his taking the son of Lydia Gage to keep till he arrives to the age of twenty one."

Those poor who were not recognized inhabitants of Lincoln were often taken back to the town from which they had come, at Lincoln's expense: "for carrying Francis Fletcher to Concord," "for carrying Mary Oliver to Woburn," "carrying Cotton Bradshir to Concord." And once Lincoln paid to have one of its own inhabitants brought back: "for the Care he took to Bring Salla Blanden from Weston to Lincoln."

Lincoln also paid for the care of the poor in their last illnesses, and for their burials: "for nursing [Margret Arpin] in her last sickness and for assisting at her funeral," "for yᵉ widow Johnson funeral," "for making a Coffing & Diging a Grave for Daniel Hager Dec.," "for diging two graves one for Wd. Gage," "for a coffin for the Widow Mary Gage," "visits to Daniel Hager in his Last Sickness," "Doctoring for Betty Loncy in her last Sickness," and "Grave for Betty Meloncy."

In addition to his treasurer's book, the treasurer of Newton, Massachusetts, kept a receipt book also.[57] Entries in it include:

Treasurer's Records

Newton Feby 27th 1766

Recd of Thomas Greenwood Esqr Town Treasurer five pounds
four Shillings out of the fine money (So Call'd), two pounds
fourteen Shillings of said Sum was what I paid to the wife of
Atherton Clark for her boarding her boy from March ye 4th 1765
to January 13th 1766; three Shillings & 4d of the aforsd Sum for a
pair of Stockings for sd Atherton Six Shillings ditto for Wood.
One pound 9/ & 4d Was for what I paid for the removal of Caleb
Child; 5/ for what I paid for the removal of the Widow Kearick.
3/7d ditto for Beulah Nardy also 6/ for what I paid for the Wido
Child in her last Sickness.

Newton Feby 27th 1766

Recd of Thomas Greenwood Esqr Town Treasurer Sixteen
Shillings & four pence for what I paid for the Support of
Atherton Clark & Family also three Shillings & 4d for what I
paid for Plowing the Ground belonging to the Work House.

Chapter Eight

Tax, Rate, and Assessor's Records

Tax lists, called Grand Lists in Vermont, are often found among town records, and they help to document the life of New Englanders in colonial times and later. New Hampshire clerks seem to have been very thorough at including tax lists in the town records, hardly missing a year in some localities. In many other New England settlements, however, such lists were not included in the town books, but were kept in separate volumes or even on loose sheets. It is not surprising, therefore, that many have become scattered. There are a number of tax lists for Rhode Island towns among the manuscripts at the Rhode Island Historical Society. Some, like that for Warwick in 1798, include the name of the owner of each piece of property with the names of abutting landowners, a description of the land and buildings, and a statement about how many windows were in the house and who occupied it. A 1778 tax list for the town of Scituate, Rhode Island, kept for many years in a drawer in the town hall, names the owner of a piece of land, and then gives the real estate (broken down by acreage under tillage and other types of land such as upland, meadow, salt marsh, and woodland); the number of cattle, oxen, goats and sheep, pigs, etc.; and various other interesting statistics, similar to the published 1771 Direct Tax of Massachusetts.[58] In Maine such land descriptions were called inventories.

Men subject to taxes were listed as "polls." A man could be taxed as early as age 16 if he owned enough real estate or personal property (generally livestock), but he would not be listed separately until he was head of his own household. Prior to this, he would be included as an extra poll in his father's household. Careful study of when men appear on tax lists can often help determine their ages and relationships to others of the same surname in town.

The early nineteenth century tax lists for Dracut, Massachusetts, show the real estate and personal estate items on which each man was taxed. In 1825 Samuel Abbot was taxed on real estate of 100 acres and buildings, and personal estate of one horse, four oxen, five cows, six swine, and one bridge share. Daniel and Josiah Ames were taxed on 66 acres and buildings, one horse, seven cows, nine swine, and one chaise. William Austin was taxed on 140 acres and buildings, six oxen, ten cows, eight swine, two horses and a colt, and one chaise.[59]

Such tax lists are frequently mistaken by novice researchers for census lists, and they do indeed give a clear picture of who owned property in town. When a tax, or "rate," was ordered by the colony or state, it was the task of the town to raise the money by an assessment on each landowner according to the property he owned. If an individual was unable to pay, he or she might receive an abatement of tax, and the lists of abatements may be helpful. A widow customarily received such relief the year her husband died; if she continued to receive one in subsequent years, probably some degree of poverty is indicated. Abatements were given also for debility, and were frequently given after wars. For example, in Reading, Massachusetts, in 1701/2, "Nathaniell Cutler Sen[r] by rason of his age and other inconvaniensis petishons the town for an Easment in his Rates it was voted and a greid that he shall be freed from his pole tax for the time to com."[60] Non-resident land owners were also included on tax lists since they had to pay taxes whether they lived in town or not; such listings often help determine when someone moved elsewhere. Tax lists are especially useful to research when a series of years is available so that names and circumstances can be compared over a long period of time.

Occasionally a non-resident would appoint a resident to be responsible for his land and taxes. On 3 August 1801 it was recorded in the Heath, Massachusetts, town book "that Thomas Stone acknowledges himself to have accepted the trust of Agent in behalf of John Lane Merchant of London and therefore considers himself as accountable for all Lawfull Taxes which may be Assessed on Land lying in the Town of Heath belonging [to] the Said John Lane during his Continuance in Said Office."[61]

Chapter Nine

Licenses

In some New England states the town had the responsibility of granting licenses for special privileges, such as the operation of "Publick houses" or "houses of Entertainment," or selling liquors. In other states this responsibility may have fallen to the county courts. In Bow, New Hampshire, on 4 March 1800 Benjamin Noyes Esq., Mr. Isaac Moor, and Mr. Jonathan Currer were each "aprobated to keep a Publick house in Bow whare he now lives by the order of the Selectmen."[62]

At a town meeting of 15 July 1719, the selectmen of Boston, Massachusetts, considered and voted the following:[63]

> The Petition of Sundry persons for Lycence to keep comon victuallin Houses and coffee House allowed by ye Sel. m. vizt. Richd Hall at his House nigh ye T. House in King Street.
>
> Robt Smith at ye House where he dwells in Summer Street.
>
> Severall p'sons Petitioning to Sell as Retailers at Large, disallowd by ye Sel. men vizt.
> Susanna Grey
> Joshua Todd & Willm Adkinson
>
> William Keens Petition to Sell Strong drink as a Retayler, allowed by ye Sel. m.
>
> John Browns Petition to Sell as an ale House nigh the Brick meeting house disallowed.
>
> Vote in addition to William Mans grant the 6th cur^t that he have also liberty to Sell Barbadose Rum by Retayl.

The selectmen of Derry, Vermont, in 1851 licensed Robert Hubbard to sell "small beer and cider" as well as "all kinds of fruit [liquors]." John M. Brigham was licensed to sell "spirituous liquors" but only for "medical, chemical and mechanical purposes."[64]

Public houses were often kept by women, sometimes the widows of previous innholders. In fact, this is one of the few occasions when women are named in town records, other than in the poor records.

By the mid-19th century some towns were beginning to license dogs. The records of Lincoln, Massachusetts, contain the following:[65]

> George Nelson has had his Dog Registered as the law requires the Name of said Dog is Jack and an English Terrier, colour Black Tan with a Strip of white in the forehead and white breast three offcet white tacs with cliped ears - 3 yrs old. 25 April 1859.

> William Millers Dog is Kept in Lincoln at David Millers, said Dog is Bull Terrier, Colour Black and Tan, Ears cliped, 3 years old -White Breast & is Licenced to be Kept in Lincoln the year ensuing Name Billy.

> Wm Mackintosh - Black Spaniel white face Spaniel no tail Name Carlow.

> Noble Thompson one Black Dog, large size, Newfoundland Breed, named Neptune.

In 1864 Marlborough, Connecticut, noted the following:[66]

> Henry Dickinson Causes to be Registered a large sized Male Dog yellow and white - named Spot.

> Adriel Huntley causes to be Registered a small sized white male dog with yellow ears two yellow spots on the right side one on the left hip - named Fiddle.

Ogden Lord Causes to be Registered a full midling sized White Male Dog with long tail - named Tiger.

And these two from North Salem, Maine, in April 1877:[67]

This certifies that Frederic Richards has caused to be registered described and numbered in the Office of the Town Clerk at Salem one yellow male dog named Carlow . . . .

License is hereby granted to Cassius M. Durrell for his dog called Geo. B. McClellan to go at large in the Streets of said Town until the 14th day of Apr. 1878 next . . . .

On 2 July 1867 according to "An Act concerning Dogs, and for the protection of Sheep and other Domestic Animals," William Cronin, police officer of Gloucester, Massachusetts, was ordered "to proceed forthwith to kill or cause to be killed all dogs within the said town not duly licensed and collared." On 2 September he reported that "I have Proceded to Kill all Dogs found unlicensed, Number of Dogs Killed two, one male Dog Owner Joseph Mitchell, and one female Dog, owner unknown."[68]

Chapter Ten

Ear or Cattle Marks and Strays

Ear marks or cattle marks are to be found in many early town records. Because most New England towns had common land, in the center of the town or elsewhere — where everyone's cattle or sheep were allowed to graze together all summer — it was important for each owner's livestock to have a distinguishing mark. Such marks usually involved a cut the size of a specific coin, combined with another cut or slit in the ear of the animal at a specified point. In Reading, Massachusetts, the mark of Samuel Lamson, recorded in 1710, was "a swallow taill in the of[f] ear and a halfpenny under the same ear."[69] Careful record of all these marks and their owners was kept by the town clerk; the Dexter, Maine, clerk in 1817 and 1818 not only recorded a written description of the ear marks, but also drew pictures of the ears and their marks.[70] Recognition of the possible genealogical value in earmarks has resulted in recent publication of such lists for Bristol, Rhode Island, in *The American Genealogist* and Foster and Scituate, Rhode Island, in *Rhode Island Roots*.[71]

Sometimes, as in Portsmouth, Rhode Island, the date was included with the information that the mark had been in use for a particular period of time. "The Ear mark of Thomas Hixes Cattel is A Slit in the Right Ear and A halfpenney under the Left Ear of one year and Seven months Standing Entred and Recorded the 30th of the 10th month 1703 [by] John Anthony Towne Cleerke."[72] This record makes it possible to pinpoint fairly exactly when Thomas Hix either arrived in town or became a freeman. Sometimes, too,

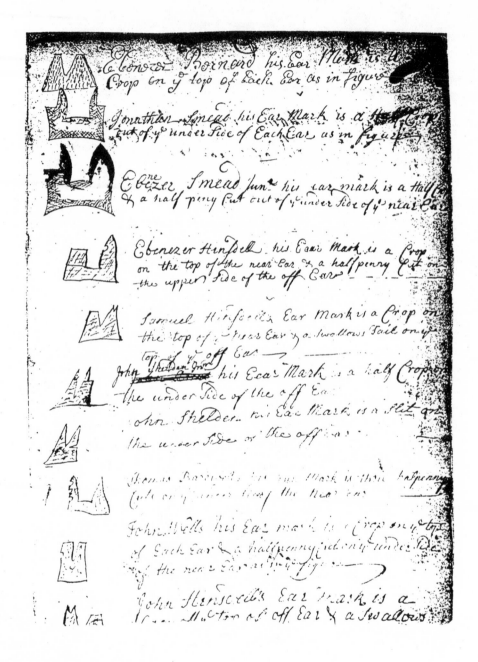

Ebenezer Barnerd his Ear Mark is a
Crop on y top of Each Ear as in figure

Jonathan Smead his Ear Mark is a Half
cut of y under side of Each Ear as in figure

Ebenezer Smead Junr his ear mark is a Half
& a half peny cut out of y under side of y near Ear

Ebenezer Hinsdell his Ear Mark is a Crop
on the top of the near Ear & a halfpenny cut on
the upper side of the off Ear

Samuel Hinsdell's Ear Mark is a Crop on
the top of y near Ear & a swallows tail on y
top of y off Ear

John Shelden Junr his Ear Mark is a half Crop on
the under side of the off Ear

John Shelden his Ear Mark is a slit cut
the under side of the off Ear

Thomas Barnerd his Ear Mark is thre halfpenny
cut on y under side y near Ear

John Wells his Ear mark is a Crop on y top
of Each Ear & a halfpenny cut on y under side
of the near Ear as in figure

John Hinsdell's Ear mark is a
Crop on y top of y off Ear & a swallows

the town clerk recorded that the earmark of a particular man was given to someone else on a certain date, indicating that the original owner had then no further need of it and had probably died or moved out of town. Occasionally such a transfer may indicate a relationship between the two owners of the mark, especially when they share a surname. In the records of Deerfield, Massachusetts, some notations seem to indicate a hereditary aspect to earmarks. On the mark originally given to John Sheldon Jr. is written "Seth Sheldon 21 Apr 1837," and then around it, "George Sheldon 18 May 1860." The mark given to Ansel Wright has written on it "George Wright 13 Feby 1856." And on the mark given to John Williams is written "Charles Williams 17 April 1841."[73]

In "Genealogical Evidence: Marks for Cattle and Sheep," Dr. Thomas H. Roderick develops evidence from the Eden, Maine, town records that the eldest son had a cattle mark that was the reverse of his father's, while a younger son had the same cattle mark as the father.[74] For example, Elisha Cousins's cattle mark was recorded as:

a crop off the left ear and a nick the under side of the right ear.

John Cousins, who was probably the eldest son of Elisha, had his mark recorded as:

a crop of the right ear and a nick the under side of the left ear

And Joseph Cousins, probably the youngest son of Elisha, had his mark recorded as:

a crop off the left ear and a nick the under side of the right

Several entries have been found that definitely show an ear mark being inherited. From Ipswich, Massachusetts:

Jacob Perkins Enters his Mark which he Derives from his Father Two half pennys on the Underside of the Near Ear.[75]

From Marlborough, Connecticut:

William Carries, March 25. 1846. Swallows tail on the Right Ear taken from his fathers mark at his decease.[76]

And from Suffield, Connecticut:

 Noah Smith 1ˢᵗ his ear mark December 21ˢᵗ 1720 which is a crop on the top of the off ear and a halfpeny Cutt in the under side of the same ear [written below in another hand] Daniel Smith has the above."[77]

The situation on Nantucket, Massachusetts, may be unique, for not only were the ear marks recorded, but so were the buying and selling of them. These examples show that ear marks were considered as part of a man's estate and as such could be both inherited and sold:[78]

Reuben Coffin yᵉ Seconds Mark which he Bought of John Colman is a flour de luce in the Left, a fork in the Right & a halpenny under it, 9 8mo 1783.

The mark that was John Swains Before he Mooved of this Place was a halpenny under Each Ear & a half take on the upper Side of the Left which after Going through Several hands is Now Paul Coggishals, 5m 16th 1786.

Daniel Allen jr Mark is a Slit in the Right Ear & a half take under the Left ordered to him by his father, 6 mo 7 1786.

Silvanus Starbucks Mark is a half take under the Right Ear & a Slit in the Left & a halfpenny over it which was his Granfathers and Now Given up to him by his Brothers in Consideration of his Quiting to them his interest in the mark that was his fathers which was a halpeny under the Lef Ear and also the above mark

Deerfield Ear Marks

without the halpenny is Taken up by Silvanus Starbuck, 5 6 mo 1788.

A halpenny undr Each Ear & a fork in the Right which was Jethro Swains mark is Sold at Auction by the administrator to his Estate to Thomas Dillano jur, 8 9 mo 1791.

Received of Barzillo Folger by the hand of Thomas Starbuck Thirty one Dollars and 67 Cents the same being in full for my Fathers Sheep and mark, Eliza Butler, 10 2 mo 1798.

By order of Enoch Coffin to mee to Enter his Sheep mark to Elizebeth Calef which Decended to him from his Father Bartlet Coffin, it being a fork in the Left and a Slope under the Right which I have Entered according to his order to his Daughter Elizebeth Clef, ye 12 ye 28 1807.

The town clerk would keep track of any strays found. It was assumed that if no one claimed the animal, it would become the property of the person who found it, or the constable of the town could sell the stray to the highest bidder after "crying" for the owner. This system also allowed the owner of a lost animal to go to the town clerk and, hopefully, be directed to the person who had found it; he was expected to pay for its keep when it was returned to him. In Reading, Massachusetts, there is a small volume titled "A Memorandum of Stray Beasts." A sample entry is the one for 10 July 1753:[79]

Taken up on ye Common Impounded and Proseaded with according to Law By Joseph Damon of Reading aforesd two Red Heifers one a Light Red the other a Deep Read Supposed to be one year old apprised one at one pound the other at Eighteen Shillings Lawfull money of New England.

Or this example from Croyden, New Hampshire, for 21 June 1824:[80]

Notice. Broke into the Inclosure of the Subscriber last Sabbath Day morning, a small brindle three years old Steer with a White Stripe in his Face, & one lopped horn, the End of which is broken. The Owner is requested to prove Property, pay Charges & take him away. Alvin Goldthwait

And sometimes the descriptions of the animals can be very detailed, as this one from Suffield, Connecticut:

October the 31st 1705 John Rising took up a stray heifer . . . is of a Black colour Cheifly: onely white all along under her tail: Her ear mark is the top of both ears taken off whether by hand or by the frost is not so easily Discernd but Cropt they are: one of the ears cropt more right over and yet a little rounding the other more rounding and comes to a peak: a little piece of one of her [horns?] either cut off or cast off whether of them it is: is Disputable off it is; which heifer we Judge to be two years old . . . And apprizd to said Rising at thirty five shillings pay; Also a horse of a black colour a star in his fore head his off hinde foot white Gray about the head no ear mark: Branded with the letter Y up one the near Buttock: with the letter H upon the nere shoulder apprizd to him at 6/8.[81]

Some towns would try to notify the owners of strays by having the town crier call them out as shown by these two examples from Simsbury and East Hartford, Connecticut:[82]

There is taken up by william Hays at Simsbury and now in his Custaty a Stray Horse of a dun culler branded with A on the nere sholder and S W on the neer hip . . . Judged to be seven years old Cryed Decem ye 6 1722 prised Decembr 20th: 1722 by Ensign phelps Samll Humphris and James Cornish Junr at Seven pounds: Entred December 21: 1722.

East Hartford July 29th 1793 I then Caused the above Described Sheep to be Cryed in East Hartford, East Windsor, & Glastenbury as the Law Directs & No Owner Appearing for them on the 6ᵗʰ Day of August 1793 I Sold at Publick Auction the whole of the aforesaid Sheep after a Beat of the Drum at a Publick Out Cry for the Sum of Nine Shillings & Nine pence and no more - Tesᵗ Nathan Monroe Constable.

Stray animals are certainly the most likely lost items to have been recorded, but one sometimes also finds personal property mentioned, such as this entry from Granby, Connecticut:

"Found by Truman Read & Now in his Custity an old morocco Bocket [*sic*] Book Contaning Twenty Nine Dollers Bank Bills & Sundry notes Payable to Marten Read Jr."[83]

East Hartford lies on the Connecticut River, and many boats, like creatures, seem to have gone astray there. Early 19th century records document the finding of a "Fish Boat, 16 feet 11 inches Long," "1 log measuring 20 feet Long and 20 inches through, marked BX," "a batteou sharp at the end 16 feet long," and "Also one other Batteau not painted no mark, an old dog rope."[84]

Chapter Eleven

Manumissions

The volume of Reading, Massachusetts, stray beasts cited in the previous section has this unusual entry at the end, dated 19 April 1776 and signed by Samuel Bancroft:

> Whereas I the Subscriber have a Negro Man Named Cato: who hath requested that he may in some future Time be made free: I hereby declare it to be my Purpose and Design that if said Cato continue an obedient and faithful Servant for the Space of three Years next after the Date hereof that at the End of said Term of three Years said Cato shall be set free.

The fire-damaged town council records of North Kingstown, Rhode Island, contain several manumissions of slaves as do the published South Kingstown town council records:[85]

> Moses Watson a Negro Man late belonging to John Watson Dec^d appeared before this Council and it is the Opinion of the Council that s^d Moses comes within the Limits of the Law for emancipating Persons held in Slavery [1791]

> Philo Peckham a Negro Man Slave late belonging to Benjamin Peckham Esqr Dec^d was this day Produced befor the Council by Josephus Peckham his Present Master and Requested the Town Council to Manumit said Philo agreeable to Law it is therefore Voted that the s^d Philo be Manumitted accordingly [1793].

Entry of freed Negroes

Whereas I the Subscriber have a
Negro-Man Named Cato: who hath
requested that he may in some [...]
Time be made free: I hereby declare
to be my Purpose and Design that [...]
said Cato continue and obedient and
faithful Servant for the Space of
three Years next after the Date [...]
that at the End of said Term of [...]
Years said Cato shall be set free

Samuel Bra[...]

April 19. 1776.

Chapter Twelve

Chattel Mortgage Books

Searching records of the early 19th century, one begins to find volumes that record the sales, mortgages, and leases of property other than land. A volume titled "Chattell Mortgage Book 1836-1839, Lynn, Massachusetts," reveals that on 22 November 1838 William Scarborough bought of Collins I. Parrott the following items: one mahogany bureau, one mahogany table, one pine table, one clock, one floor carpet, and one looking glass, for a total of $50.00. Scarborough paid $10.00 in cash and signed a 90-day note for the remaining $40.00.[86]

In a similar volume for the town of Burlington, Massachusetts, there is an unusual mortgage. Benson Clark, a tavern keeper, on 20 February 1837, mortgaged for $700 the contents of his tavern, including

> 1 Secretary, 6 Tables, 3 Toilet tables, 5 Looking glasses, 2 work Tables, Crockery and Tinware, 8 Bed steds, 8 Beds and Beding, 1 Time piece, 2 Carpets and Rugs, [Charts?] and pictures, Sundry Books, Hollow ware and Kitchen furniture, 4 [dozen?] Chairs, 3 fire Setts, 1 Mattress, 2 Stoves, Box furniture, a Sign, Chaise saddle Bridle and harness, wagon, and one hog.

Clark noted that "All the foregoing property is in and abot my Tavern," though we are told that, fortunately, "the hog [is] in my barn."[87]

These sales and leases did not always involve cash, but might be based on the natural increase of the livestock. The Hersey, Maine, town records contain the following lease on 20 May 1872:[88]

This is to certify I Leslie Tozier of Dayton Pl[antation] [now Hersey] do this Day Lease to Charles H. Noyes of Dayton Pl. the following described Cow to wit: one brindle & white cow six years old this summer the same I bought of E.S. Morse, that the same are free from all Incumbrences, to have & to for the term of four years from the date hereof.

At which time the said Noyes is to return said cow & a heiffer in payment for the use of said Cow.

These mortgage books may include any property — except for land — including ships. William A. Emmons of Gorham, Maine, in 1846 mortgaged the Schooner *Emerald* " . . . built at Vassellborough and emploid in the coasting business between Portland & Boston, purchased by me of Henry Williams at Augusta and now at sea."[89]

Like deeds for land, the chattel mortgage records sometimes indicate family relationships. Russell Linnell of Gorham sold "all my right title and interest in and to all of the personal property of the late Samuel Linnell . . . the same personal estate being subject to the use and occupancy of the Widow of the said Samuel for and during her natural life. . . ." The exact relationship between Russell and Samuel is not given, but they were probably father and son.[90]

As is the case in probate inventories, when mortgages or sales involved household items, the property is often described room by room. James McArthur of Gorham mortgaged "all the furniture now in the house occupied by me in said Gorham." The furniture is organized "in Western front room," "in front Entry," "in Eastern front Room," "in Eastern chamber," "in Western Chamber," "in Chamber Bed Room," "in Actic Story," and in "the Barn."[91]

Chapter Thirteen

School Records

School matters also were a part of town business. Rarely do school records include information on the children attending school; rather they are concerned with finding and engaging school teachers and paying them, the minutes of the school committee meetings, and upkeep of the school house. In Hatfield, Massachusetts, on 4 March 1705/6, Thomas Hastings Jr. was voted to keep school for £35, "One third part . . . in Merchantable Rye: One third part in Indian Corn (Merchantable) and the other third part in Merchantable Barley and Oats."[92] In Reading, Massachusetts, in 1720, Mr. Thomas Oliver was appointed schoolmaster:[93]

> . . . to keep a school in the town of Reading . . . for the term of
> one year . . . to begin on the 25th of this instant April . . . and so
> to be until a whole year to be ended . . . and the said Oliver doth
> promise and engage diligent and faithfully to attend the
> seasonable hours of schooling and will use his utmost endeavour
> to teach and instruct the children to read and write and cypher.
> And the selectmen of Reading do promise for themselves . . . in
> behalf of the town . . . the sum of 43 pounds in current passable
> money to be paid quarterly.

A century later in the Reading records one finds a list of the books in the school house.

In 1729 in Hatfield, Massachusetts, it was voted:[94]

> that every parent or master in the Town, that shall send any
> children or servant to the school, are obliged to procure one half
> a load of wood to each Scholar . . . And that if any parent or

Master shall neglect to carry wood . . . their children or servants
shall be debarred of any privilege of the fire in said School until
their parents or Masters do procure wood.

As towns grew, many were divided into several school districts.
On 20 February 1797 Croyden, New Hampshire, chose "a
Committee to squardron out the Town for the Use of Schooling or
make any Alteration to the Squardrons as they now stand."[95] And
when Montville, Maine, was divided into school districts in 1807,
the heads of families in each district were listed with the number of
children in each household.[96] This list is particularly interesting in
that all heads of households are listed, even those with no school
age children, as shown by the following for District No. 1:

Name	Children
James Bagley	2
Joseph Cromwell	1
Joseph Levitt	2
[Smith?] Cram	8
Richard Small	0
Daniel Meservey	0
Sam¹ Gage	0
Levi Bagley	2
Baptick Gillmore	0
Sam¹ Moores	2
Wᵐ Mcmaster	1
Phinehas Everett	1
Ebenezar Everett	0
John Miliken	7
Rufus Carter	3
Perley Ayer	4
Ezekiel True	5
Ebenezar Stevens	0
Stephen Prescott	4

Woodstock, Maine, was also divided into school districts by family:[97]

> The Families of Lemuel Perham Lemuel Perham Jun[r] Rowse Bisbee Jotham Perham Thomas Farrer Joseph Whitman Joseph Clefford John Billings Edward Lothrop Merrill Chase and Noah Curtis Jun[r] together with all such as may hereafter come within the limits of said District Shall Constitute one Destrict and be called The first school Destrict

> The families of John Gray Jun[r] Benjamin Fobes Lazarus Rand George Townsend Josiah Dudley John Starberd Daniel Doey & John Lunt together with all such as may hereafter come within the limits of said District shall constitute one Destrict and be called the fifth School Destrict

Occasionally one finds information about the students themselves in the town's school records. In the 1830s, Derby, Vermont, listed heads of households with the number of children over four and under eighteen, like Croyden, New Hampshire, above. By the 1850s such lists included not only the head of household, but also the names of all the children in each household, such as Josiah Streetter with Arvilla, Oscar, Edmund, and Emeline, or Wm. R. Spear with Mae E., Ellen S., and Ann Taylor.[98]

The Corbin Collection at the New England Historic Genealogical Society contains manuscript copies from Brimfield, Massachusetts, of a "List of Scholars in Free Grammar School 1855-1868" and "Hitchcock Free High School, Admission Applications, 1874-1886." The lists of scholars for the Grammar School for many of the years include the students' names, ages, and residences, and for one year, 1857, their dates of birth. It is interesting that this school drew students not only from Brimfield but also from surrounding towns such as Amherst, Sturbridge, and Warren in Massachusetts, and Woodstock in Connecticut.

Each Hitchcock admission application for high school students includes the name of applicant, date of birth, age, residence, place of birth, and name of father and mother. For example, George H. Haynes was born at Sturbridge on 20 March 1866, was 12 years 5 months of age, the son of Henry D. and Lizzie C. Haynes. Like the Free Grammar School, Hitchcock School drew its students from a wide area surrounding Brimfield. Places of residence given in the first fifty applications include Brimfield, Brookfield, Cambridgeport, Fiskdale, Greenwich, Hardwick, Holland, Orange, Palmer, South Wilbraham, Sturbridge, Wales, Warren, and West Brookfield in Massachusetts; Camden, Maine; and Jewett City, Connecticut. Birthplaces included Bloomington, Illinois; Brattleboro, Vermont; Camden, Maine; Boston, Brimfield, East Brimfield, Greenwich, Holden, Holland, Lancaster, New Braintree, North Brookfield, Palmer, Paxton, Shelbourn Falls, South Wilbraham, Springfield, and Wales, Massachusetts; Woodstock, Connecticut; Providence, Rhode Island; New York; and Hillsburg and Lakeville, Nova Scotia.

Chapter Fourteen

Military Records

Military information may appear in the town records in many different forms. There may be rolls and rosters of the town militia, or lists of payments for military service among the treasurer's records. The way in which a man is mentioned in the records may indicate his participation in the militia. In Reading, Massachusetts, Jeremiah Swaine was first called Captain in 1677 and continued so until 1690 when he was styled Major, a title he bore for another twenty years until his death. Such titles most likely refer to the town militia rather than to service on the colony level.

Groton, Massachusetts, has a large collection of receipts from men who received their bounty for Revolutionary service. One receipt, dated 4 August 1777, contains the signatures of thirteen men, and marks of two others, who received 12 shillings each as bounty from the town. An unusual receipt in this collection, dated on one side at Cambridge, Massachusetts, 11 February 1778, states that

> Mr. Mich[l] Keveain a Ressidant in this town for one year, and
> haith behav[d] himself respectifull, and well among us & having an
> inclination to go in the publect Service against our Enimies, that
> we have in this Town our full Qota of men for the three years
> Ca[m]ppain Latly ordered by the Great & Gen[ll] Court of this
> State.

The reverse side, dated at Groton, 14 February 1778, states that

> I hereby acknowledge myself to have inlisted into the
> Continental army for the Term of Three years . . . as a Soldier in
> Cap[t] Sylvanus Smiths Company and Col[o] Bigelows Regt to make
> up the Quota assigned the Town of Groton . . . & have this Day

received of Capt Benj^a Bancroft Town Treasurer . . . the sum of sixty pounds . . . as a Bounty for s^d Service. [*signed*] Michael Keenin[99]

The records of Sherburn, Massachusetts, include a copy of a bill sent to General Phipps, one of a committee for hiring men into the Service in 1778. It lists amounts for the time that went into hiring Elias Grout for Continental service, Jeremy Lealand for service to the North River, Timothy Kendall to go to Providence, fourteen men for an expedition to Rhode Island, procuring three men to guard the Convention Troops at Cambridge, and "a journey to Boston to Try to obtain liberty of Genl Heath that the men . . . here might be Stationed at ye Continental Store in this Town which would have Saved ye Town a Considerable Sum."[100]

In Lincoln, Massachusetts, a volume titled "The Book of the Treasurer's Accompts in Lincoln 1755" includes payment to many men, beginning in 1776. Typical is one dated 19 February 1776, "Paid to Mr Willard Parks Eighteen Shillings for a Sett of Accoutriments as a Minute Man . . ." or this one of 24 July 1776: "Paid to Mr Eleazer Parks Eleven Shillings for one Baonet on ram-rod & knap Sack which he found for him self as a minute man so Called.[101]

Reading, Massachusetts, also paid for minute men, but as the following examples show, the payments were not always made to the man who served:[102]

12 October 1776: Joseph Hill 20/ for his sons Joseph & James serving as minet men ten days.

17 October 1776: Thomas Taylor Jr 13/ it being for Luke Richardsons serving 6 days & half as a minute man.

4 March 1777: Edmond Eaton 22/ for Eleven Days Service himself & Amos Briant as minet men.

3 October 1777: Capt John Walton 11/ for 5 days & half Service of Apprintce Isaac Walton as minute man.

In 1835 several depositions were entered in the records of Acton, Massachusetts, concerning the death of Captain Isaac Davis at Concord on 19 April 1775. His widow stated:[103]

I Hannah Leighton of Acton testafy, that I am eighty nine years of age. Isaac Davis who was killed in the Concord Fight in 1775 was my husband. He was then thirty years of age. We had four Children the youngest about fifteen months old. They were all unwell when he left me in the morning some of them with the canker rash. The alarm was given early in the morning and my husband lost no time in making ready to go to Concord with his company . . . My husband said but little that morning. He seemed serious and thoughtful but never seemed to hesitate as to the course of his duty.

One of the accompanying depositions began:

I Thomas Thorp of Acton testify that I am in my eightieth year and have lived here ever since I was fifteen years old. I was a member of Capt Isaac Davis's Company which was formed in November 1774. We usually met twice a week for drill. Capt. Davis was a gunsmith. He was esteemed a man of courage and prudence and had the love and veneration of all his company.

The effects of war may be seen in the town records in ways other than in the actual listings of soldiers. In 1776 many towns recorded verbatim the Declaration of Independence. At an Ashby, Massachusetts, town meeting of 25 February 1777, "in order to Determine & affix the Price of the following Articles Nesessary for the support of Life and Trade," prices were set for every conceivable work and commodity. Farm labor from 20 June to 20 August was set at three shillings per day, and from the middle of

November to the middle of March at one shilling. Labor for the rest of the year was to be "in Proportion to the above prices as usual." Good wheat was fixed at 6s 8d per bushell, good rye at 4s 4d, and good Indian corn at 3s 4d. Raw hides were fixed at three pence a pound and green calf hides at sixpence a pound. Good yarn stockings and good leather shoes for men were fixed at six shillings each; other shoes "in Proportion to their Begness & Quallity."[104]

Other towns passed resolves to support the resistance to the British Acts. Article Five of a resolution passed in New Braintree, Massachusetts, on 2 September 1774 states:

> we will not Either by our selves or any for or under us buy or sell or use any of ye East India Companys Tea Imported from Great Brittain or any other Tea with a Duty for Raising a Revanue thereon in amarica which is affixt By act of Parliment on the Same; Neither will we suffer any such Tea to be made use of in any of our families.

Five weeks later the town voted "that Seven men be . . . Chosen a Committee to Inspect all Tea Drinkers and Consumers of East India Tea and to post their names."[105]

The following resolve for March 1774 from Hinsdale, New Hampshire, serves to remind us that not everyone was caught up in the political fury preceding the Revolutionary War:[106]

> . . . after Finishing the Necessary Business of the Town, the day not being fully Spent the Town took into Consideration many Patriotic Speeches & Pompous Declamations with which The News Papers are Continually Interlarded wherein the Rights & Liberties of the Peoples of this Country are Represented to be invaded & the English Constitution Thereby in Danger of being wholly broken up, and also the Resolutions of many Towns in New England Respecting the Rights and Liberties before mentioned and finding that it is become very Fashionable for Towns

to Enter in to Resolutions Respecting their Rights & Libertis & Recollecting the Old Proverb that it wou'd be as well to be out of the World as out of the Fashion were Induced to Resolve as Follows —

1. Resolved as the Opinion of this Town that it is the Indispensable duty of every member of Society haveing Certain Knowledge what Rights & Priveledges appertain to him to Exert himself to Preserve those Rights and Priveledges whenever they are in danger of being Wrested from him but until he Knows what Rights and Priveleges belong to him he ought not to Interpose in Political Matters but industriously persue the Common & Ordinary Business of his Calling & Endeavour to Cultivate Urbanity & Social Harmony.

2. It is the Opinion of this Town that true personal Liberty (so much Contended for) Consists in the Right every member of Society hath in going when & Where he likes in Persuit of that which best pleaseth him (without being Tar'd or Feather'd therfor) so Long as he Conforms to the Laws of Society . . . .

3d. It is the Opinion of this Town that the Tumult which now prevails in this Country Respecting the East India Companys sending their Tea here for Sale does not Arise by Reason of the Acts of Parliament wich imposes a duty on Tea for the Purpose of Raiseing a Revennue but because the Intended method of Sale in this Country by yᵉ East India Company woud probably hurt the private Intrest of many Persons who deal largely in Tea . . . there are other Acts of Parliament . . . which Infringe the Rights and Liberties of the People . . . Yet no Objection is made . . . .

4th. Resolved, that the Consequences Attending the use of New England Rum are much More Pernicious to Society than the Consequences attending the use of Tea for Altho Tea hath been Represented to be the most destructive and Poisinous Thing in use & hath deprived Hundreds of the good People of this Country of their Lives . . . Yet it is Evident that New England Rum is much more destructive and hath and ever Will while used in such Abundance destroy the lives & Liberties of thousands . . . .

5thly. It is the Opinion of this Town that if those Patriotic Persons and Towns who declaim so loudly against the Use of Tea and in Defence of the Rights of their Country woud promote the True Intrest Thereof By Banishing New England Rum the Greatest Evil with which this Country was Ever Infested this Town Will in Return Endeavour to Banish from them the Use of that Tea which hath been Impeach'd of being unhealthy & unConstitutional.

6thly. It is the Opinion of this Town that if half the Time that is Idly Spent in hearing Lectures from Patriotic Enthusiasts was Spent in promoteing Peace Harmony & good order in Cultivateing the Lands and in Encourageing Industry & Agriculture it woud add Greatly to the True Intrest of this Country.

7thly. It is the Opinion of this Town that under the disguise of Patriotism, that first Rate Virtue, Factive Self Intrest and private Ambition are frequently Conceal'd, and that many Persons who Pretend to be Patriots and declaim Loudly in Defence of the Rights of their Country are bound by no Ties but those of Partial Passion and private Intrest, but Yet so Artfully Conceal themselves under the disguise of Patriotism that it Requires more than Common Penetration to Discover the Delusion.

8thly. It is the Opinion of this Town that the True dignity and Glory the Stability and Internal Tranquility of Every State were always Proportioned to the Strength & Diffusiveness of Publick Spirit and that the Noisy Intemperate froth of a political Enthusiast is as Far Removed from a Steady Principle of Patriotism as ye Dignity of Solid understanding from the Fam[*torn*] of Poetical Madness.

The records of Groton, Massachusetts, contain information on Shays' Rebellion, including Oaths of Allegiance which the participants were required to take afterwards. One dated at Harvard, Massachusetts, 20 March 1787, lists not only the men's names, but their occupations:[107]

Joseph Wetherbee of Groton Blacksmith
Ebenezer Farnsworth of Groton Laborer
Abel Wetherbee of Groton Laborer
Eleazer Davis of Groton Cordwainer
Abel Morse of Groton Wheelwright
Jesse Stone of Groton Laborer
Abel Davis Junr of Groton a miner
Ben^j Frost of Groton a miner
Timothy Stone of Groton a miner
Joseph Park of Groton yeoman
John Moore of Groton yeoman
John Park of Groton Stone cutter

New Braintree, Massachusetts, on 23 March 1787 recorded the following men who rebelled, then took the oath of allegiance:[108]

. . . Phinehas Warner Junr, Harlow Barnaby, John Gardner, James Barr, John Barr Junr, Samuel Bowker & John Blair Junr all of New Braintree . . . came before me surrendered up their Arms & took and subscribed the Oath of Allegiance . . . also Joseph Swinnerton, Stephen Pepper, Elijah Mason, Alpheus Warner, Tim° Shaw, Noah Grainger, John Pepper, Josiah Gilbert, Webster Hayford Junr, Jonathan Hayford, William Thomson, Moses Whipple, Silas Bigelow Thomson, and Josiah Henderson all of New Braintree . . . came before me and took and Subscribed the Oath of Allegiance . . . but Delivered up no arms, the reasons assigned are as Follows, Swinnerton says he had a Borrowed Gun, & cannot procure one to Deliver up, Stephen and John Pepper says their Guns were left Near Springfield & Supposed to be fell into the hands of men in the Government Service, Elijah Mason says he was a Fifer & never took up arms, Alph^s Warner Noah Grainger Tim° Shaw, Webster Halford J^r & Jon^a Halford - Wm Thomson Silas B. Thomson were Excused from Delivering up arms by Col° Timothy Newell the Commanding officer in Government Service Stationed in this Town, Moses Whipple says he never Bore arms against Government, but acted as a Drummer,

> Josiah Gilbert being a Minor took a Gun privatly without his
> masters leave, and was he says Excused Delivering arms by L^t
> Samson Witherell an officer in Col° Newells Reg^t, & Josiah
> Henderson was taken up in this Town by Col° Eben^r Crafts and
> his arms carried away by the said Col° Crafts and his party of
> Light Horsemen. . . .

For the Civil War, there may also be rosters of militia men. Such a list from Cary, Maine, made in 1862, not only gives the names of the militia men, but also their ages and for many of them, dates of birth. The men range in age from 18 to 45.[109]

Many Massachusetts towns kept volumes called Rebellion Records listing Civil War soldiers. Dighton has a volume labeled "Rebellion Record, Volume 1, 1863" on the cover and "Record of Soldiers and Officers in the Military Service" on the title page. The printed headings across the double page are "Name & residence, Time & Place of birth, When Enlisted, When Mustered, Rank, Enlisted for [months or years], Regiment, Company, Bounty, Single or Married, Names of Parents, Previous occupations, Promotions, Resignations, Discharges, Deaths, etc." While not every column is filled in for each soldier, the following examples show that quite a lot of information is contained in the volume:[110]

> Elhanan Ingalls, born in Dighton, mustered 11 June 1861 for 3
> years, in the 7th Regiment Company H, paid $15 bounty, single,
> son of Allen H. and Lydia, occupation Mason, Deserted 1
> January 1863, reenlisted in New York Regiment, wounded and
> discharged.

> John H. Pitts, born in Dighton, mustered 11 June 1861 for 3
> years, in the 7th Regiment Company C, paid $15 bounty, single,
> son of Henry and Sarah, occupation Shoemaker, reenlisted 1864
> [written above this was] Mortally Wounded.

James L. Gay, born in Dighton, mustered 11 June 1861 for 3 years, in the 7th Regiment Company D, paid $15 bounty, single, son of Charles, died 19 August 1862.

Benjamin P. Jones, born in Dighton 21 July 1814, mustered 3 September 1862 for 3 years, in the 40th Regiment Company D, paid $325 bounty, married, son of Jonathan and Hannah, occupation Farmer, died in Hospital at Bermuda Hundredths, Virginia, 9 January 1865 of Fever.

Arthur A. Hathaway, born in Dighton 26 November 1847, mustered 3 September 1864 for 1 year, in the 2d. H.A., paid $400 bounty, son of Isaac and Elizabeth.

Shrewsbury, Massachusetts, has a "Rebellion Record," filled in more completely than the Dighton volume. It is noteworthy that the men enlisting from Shrewsbury were born in 38 different places. Massachusetts places of birth were: Athol, Attleborough, Auburn, Belchertown, Boylston, Brimfield, Grafton, Holliston, Millbury, Newburyport, Northborough, Oakham, Shrewsbury, Southborough, South Boston, Springfield, Sterling, Sudbury, Ware, Westborough, and Worcester. Other birthplaces were: Fitzwilliam and Hancock, New Hampshire; Farrington, Bridgston, Machias and Phillips, Maine; Danville, Newfane, and Montpelier, Vermont; Albany, and East Constable, New York; Truro, Nova Scotia, Montreal, Canada, Township of Clark, Canada West; Co. Galway, Ireland; and Banbury, Oxfordshire, England.

At the end of this volume is a list of men known to be alive on 12 February 1909, the 100th anniversary of the birth of Abraham Lincoln, including "Harrison Maynard, just removed to California." The list is followed by the death dates for several of these men, from 1910 to 1916.

Chapter Fifteen

Poor Records

While it is certainly worthwhile to study town records in order to flesh out the bare facts of the life of someone who lived in a colonial town and owned land there, the rewards of a search for a poverty-stricken person or family may be even greater. The town was, as we have seen, a small welfare state, and in its dealings with the poor or ill, one sometimes finds the only evidence available to identify a person who lived there or who perhaps wandered in from another town. In 1734 the selectmen of Ipswich, Massachusetts, directed Capt. Thomas Wade, overseer of the poor, to "make Suitable provision for the poor for the necessarys of Life . . . that the poor be also provided for and kept together in a Suitable & convenient House . . . to employ such of the poor as are capable of labour."[111]

The town of Acton, Massachusetts, on 9 April 1824 spelled out the duties incumbent upon the overseers of the poor:[112]

> What they will support all those persons that are wholly or partly supported and all those persons that may apply for assistance and all those persons that may be Brought from any other town to the under taker that belong to this Town for support for one year from the above Date.
>
> To be supported in evry respect to free the town from all expence of boarding, Clothing, Doctoring, nurseing, and evry expence in sickness and health funeral expences included. And all those persons that may need assistance in this town the under taker shall take them immediately on either of the overseers notifying him of assistance being wanted and no expence to the under taker before notice is given and all those that are wholly

supported their Clothes to be kept in as good repair as they find
them all those that are under eighteen years of age shall have as
good Supply of schooling as other Children have of that age. On
Complaint of any persons the overseers will Consider it their
Duty to see that they are well used in evry respect.

Following practice long established in England, towns took care
of their own poor, but resisted assuming responsibility for anybody
else. If a "transient" appeared in town, perhaps as a guest of one of
the inhabitants, his presence was duly noted by the town council
(in Rhode Island), or the selectmen (in the other New England
states). Shortly thereafter, the transient might be ordered to leave
town, or to give evidence about his or her last place of legal
settlement.

The order to leave town was called a "warning out." (For a more
complete discussion, see Josiah Henry Benton, *Warning Out in
New England* [Boston, 1911; reprint Bowie, Md.: Heritage Books,
1992].) The warning did not mean that the visitors must
immediately leave town, but simply informed them that the town
would not support them if for any reason they should become
unable to do so themselves. On 28 December 1764 the selectmen of
Salem, New Hampshire, delivered a warrant to Evan Jones,
constable, "to warn out of this town Tim^y Kezzer & Marcy his wife
& Five Children (viz) Mary & Samuel Moses & Anna & David
[t]heir Children who Came from the town of Haverhill to this
town in ye month of Novr Last Past." On the same day he also
warned "Rebackah Woodbury who Came from the town of New
Port in ye Prov^e of Rhod Iland."[113]

The following warning out comes from Andover, Vermont:[114]

To either Constable of Andover in the County of Windsor -
Greeting You are hereby required to summons Jonathan Winn
and Mary Winn his wife and susannah Clarisa Asa Polly Betsey
and Hannah their children, now residing in Andover to depart sd
town. . . .

Samuel Clark on 28 February 1815 stated that he "served this
precept by delivering a true and attested Coppy of the original with
my return here on thereon endorsed into the hands of the within
named Susannah Winn." Apparently he served the notice on one of
the children!

Alden M. Rollins of the University of Alaska has recently
published the first volume of his ongoing work, *Vermont Warnings
Out* (Camden, Me.: Picton Press, 1995), abstracting such records for
all towns in ten counties in northern Vermont. The rest of the
state will be covered in future volumes. In an introduction Mr.
Rollins provides a useful discussion of the custom of warning out,
and a bibliography for further reading.

Other records that are similar in content to warnings out, but
less common, are notifications submitted to the town clerk by
inhabitants, indicating that they had taken non-residents into their
homes. Here are a few examples from such a volume for Weston,
Massachusetts:[115]

I have taken into my Service & to Dwell here with me in Weston
for the Space of a month a molatto man free Born named
Ebenezer Way who was Lately a Resident at Sauco or Biddeford
as he Says Born at Boston that he may be warned out of this
town if occasion should Require it as I understand by him he was
Lately warned out of Boston he Began his Service with me the
ninth of this Present month I am yours Joseph Roberts Weston
July 22 1767.

I have taken into my Faimely in march Last one Daniel Whitney he Came from Sudbury he is about Seaven years old yours Joseph Whitney Weston April 15:1771.

... that the 24 of april 1771 I took into my House Jacob Baker with his Wife Hannah and one Child Jacob from Lincon Elisabeth Hager.

I have taken into my House to Dwell John Stedman and Sarah his Wife & Sarah his Daughter and Margret alis Pegey William and John there Children they Came from Newton and Came here the Sixteenth Day of April Last Weston June 20 1774 Benjamin Peirce.

I have Hirred as a Jorneyman into my Service one John Munn a Hatter by Traid he Came to me the 6 Day of May last he Came from Boston to me his Circumstances very Low Weston Sept 12:1774 John Pownall.

In 1786 the Natick, Massachusetts, town clerk made "An account Such Families and Persons as has Mov^d into Natick this year." Included were "Mrs Barker & one child named John last from Milford and Mr Barker formerly from Boston," "Speedwell Allen Negro and family from Boston," "Tomas Russell and Abigail his wife and Daniel, Thomas, and Shubal their Children from Sherborn," and "Joseph Worsely and wife from Brookline."[116] In 1791 the Cambridge, Massachusetts, town clerk wrote "The following list contains an exact return of people resideing in the town of Cambridge A.D. 1791 who at that time had never gained an inhabitancy in said Town." It included "Solomon Bowman & Abigail his Wife with Three children viz Elizabeth Sibbel & Polly, last from Lexington" and "William Cox & Susannah his Wife, Foreigners."[117] The term "foreigner" may not have meant that William and Susannah Cox were from another country, but rather that they came from another town or state. No indication is given as to whether these persons were ever actually warned out or not.

Later in this same Cambridge volume is recorded "To the Selectmen of town of Cambridge Gentlemen The Subscriber has in the employment of the University the following persons who lodge at his house." These employees included:

Peter Waters a blackman born in Maryland served in the American Army in the late war, afterwards lived in Newton & from thence came into the Subscribers employment March 15th 1789.

Hannah Dickson, aged 42 born in Cambridge, removed to Medford when six years old, which has since been the place of her residence she entered into the Subscribers employment August 11 1789. She spends the vacation at Medford at her home.

Pompey Parsons a blackman aged 42 brought from Africa when ten years old. Immediately after his arrival went to live with the Rev[d] M[r] Parsons of Bradford with whom he continued two or three years, till his masters death; after which he was under the care of Dr Scott of Boston, till 21 years old which town Boston he has since considered as the place of his residence. He came unto the Subscribers service the 13th of last month.

In some towns inhabitants were required to post bonds for the non-residents they sheltered. One such example comes from Woburn, Massachusetts:[118]

7: of 3 mo 1677

called Ralph Read to acoumpt for Entertaining Joseph Blud who with John Johnson Entered into bond as followeth

Know all men by these presents that wee John Johnson and Ralph Read bind our selves heirs and Executors in a bond of twenty pounds a year to bee paid to Frances kendall one the

Towns behalfe at or before the last of Agust next insueing this
date The Conditions of the above written obligation is such that
in case the said John Johnson and Ralph Read beare all charges
that may come to this Towne by Entertaining Joseph Blud then
this bond to bee voyd . . . .

At meetings in January and February 1698/9, "relating to John
pelham his Intruding himself into towne," John Carter Sr. refused
to give the Woburn selectmen a bond. Carter "denyed that he
Either Entertained him as an Inmate, or had leased any hous or
land to him." The town decided that since Pelham had been legally
warned from town, he must leave, or his case would be appealed to
the court of General Sessions.[119]

In 1820, complaint was made to the town council of
Cumberland, Rhode Island, that Ruth Strange, wife of John
Strange, a transient person, was now chargeable to the town.[120]
Ruth was called before the council, where she declared that before
her marriage she was Ruth Thurber, born in Rehoboth in the State
of Massachusetts, was in her twenty-sixth year when she married
John Strange in Warren, and that they lived in Swanzey when they
first began to keep house, which was after her husband came home
from the Army. She described several moves between Swanzey,
Rehoboth, and Dartmouth, then Warren and finally Attleborough,
and said that her husband had never owned any real estate. It
remains a mystery why the town council decided that her last legal
settlement was Portsmouth, to which they ordered her removed.

A landless transient in Rhode Island, when served with a
warning out, was often able to produce a certificate from his home
town, stating that he was a legal resident there and would be taken
back at any time. Individuals planning a move might ask their town

council in advance for these certificates of residence, which would be addressed to the council of the new town. Quite often a man's certificate would include the names of his wife and children. One finds these documents most often in the records of the towns where people attempted to settle, and less often in the records of the towns that issued them.

Newport, Rhode Island, has a small book, now in fragmentary condition, in which only certificates of residence were recorded. In most towns, however, these are thoroughly mixed in with other business. In South Kingstown, Rhode Island, a number of loose certificates were recently discovered among other unbound papers dating back to the early 1700s.

If the town council determined that an individual was likely to become chargeable to the town and need assistance, it usually proceeded to order the constable to carry the unhappy wanderer back to the last place of legal settlement. The payment for this was usually recorded, giving at least an approximate day for the forcible removal, and a search can thus be extended to another town in the hope of continuing the story in the records there.

The following two examples are from South Kingstown, Rhode Island:[121]

> Voted that Prudence R. Sheffield have a Certificate to Remove to New Shoreham in the County of Newport acknowledging Her to be legally Settled in this Town at this time and that this Town will Receive Her at any time whenever she shall be sent without any expence to this Town . . . .

> Voted that this Town Council do not Receive Rowse Card Wife nor Child about three Months old. Voted that whereas the above Named Rowse Card his Wife Elisabeth and Child about three Months old are now in this Town & likely to become chargeable

& by a Certificate from the Town of Charlestown . . . it appears
that said Charlestown was the last legal place of Settlement of said
Rowse Card Wife & Child . . . Whereupon this Council do
adjudge & determine that s^d Charlestown was and now is the legal
place of Settlement of said Rowse Card . . . and that an Order be
forthwith Issued Signed by the Clerk of this Council to Remove
said Rowse Card Wife and Child to said Charlestown and them
deliver to the overseers of the Poor . . . .

If illness or misfortune struck down someone who belonged to
the town (that is, someone legally born there to parents who
enjoyed legal settlement), the person concerned might apply to the
town council or selectmen for help. The town might then supply
provisions or clothing, or, in cases of more severe debility, might
arrange for the afflicted person to move in with another resident,
who would be paid monthly for his or her upkeep. Such payments
were regularly recorded in the town treasurer's records. In 1774 the
town of Athol, Massachusetts, "granted eight pounds thirteen
shillings and four pence to pay Simon Goddard for the bringing up
of Thomas Woods a poor child put to him by the Selectmen."[122] In
1791 Susannah Miller was paid by the town of Reading,
Massachusetts, "for Cloathing her Children" and "for Boarding her
Children."[123] Or the town might compel family members to take
care of the poor person: On 13 April 1721 the town of Simsbury,
Connecticut, voted to take "an action against the Children of
widdow Gillit Relict of Ammiah Gillit of Simsbury deceasd in
order to Charg them with her maintenance according to Law."[124]

The "Selectmen records 1828-1857" for Ashby, Massachusetts,
contain a year by year inventory from 1841 to 1850 of the
possessions, mainly clothing, of each of the town's paupers.[125] On
9 April 1842, Sumner Willington, aged 6, had a cotton frock and

pantaloons (too small), two shirts, one pair of socks, one pair of old boots, a woollen spencer and pantaloons, two old aprons, and one old cap. His sister, Lucy, aged 7, had two calico dresses (one good), three aprons (good), two shirts, one pair of shoes, one pair of stockings, one summer bonnet, one straw bonnet, and two petticoats.

Some towns actually auctioned off the poor. In 1840, Brooksville, Maine,

> "Next voted to put the poor at auction to be supported by the Lowest bidder and the children to be Bound Boys until twenty one Girls until Eighteen years old the Sum to be Divided into equal paments and paid each pament annually until the sum is paid for which they may Bed off."[126]

Amaziah D. Blake bid $49 for keeping Mehitable Woodbridge for one year, Daniel McGee bid $26 for Sarah Webber, and Abner Gray bid just $10 for Mrs. Eaton and her youngest child. The Kench family had fallen on hard times, probably after the death of the father since he is not mentioned in this list. Avery Gray bid to take Mrs. Kench and her youngest child. William Kench was bound to N. N. Tibbetts and Robert Kench to Luther Bates, each until they reached the age of 21, and Mary Kench was bound to Richard Condon until she became 18. Hannah Kench was left with the overseers of the poor.

These bids can vary greatly even for the same person during the space of a single year. This may indicate that their skill or craft was of a seasonal nature. In Chittenden, Vermont, Aaron Beach was bid off to Phinehas Clark for the first three months at $1.34 per week, to Seth Churchell for the second three months at $.83 per week, to

Jonathan Keith for the third quarter at $.73 per week, and to Elijah Seger for the fourth quarter at $1.00 per week.[127]

Searching out these references to the poor in the town treasurer's records often requires patience and perseverance, for they are buried in the records of other town business, as shown in an earlier example under Treasurer's Records. However, such a search may provide information not available anywhere else. In the treasurer's records of Natick, Massachusetts, there are deaths not recorded in the published vital records. The death of Samuel Stratton Senior is listed as having occurred on 17 December 1789.[128] A *Book of Strattons* states that Samuel[4] Stratton (*Samuel³, John², Samuel¹*) was born in Watertown in 1703, married there, and had children recorded from 1727 through 1750.[129] This same source says that this Samuel bought land in Natick in 1759 and that his son was the Samuel Stratton Jr. who was warned out of Natick in 1765. But the compilers of this genealogy missed the fact that Samuel[4] died in Natick in 1789.

The "Townsend [Massachusetts] Pauper Book" notes that on 22 December 1830 Joel Emery "made application to have something done for" Edward McBride. On 15 October 1834 the book notes that "Edward McBride says - He came from Montreall June 19 - 1830 -Born in Coagh in the County of Teyrone - Ireland aged about 45 -years." The death of Edward McBride at the Poor Farm was entered on 10 February 1835.[130]

The list of 7 April 1794 of "Poor put out for one year" for Natick, Massachusetts, records "Ceasar Ferrit & wife to Adam Bullard for" 15 shillings.[131] The death of Ceasar Ferrit is recorded in the published Natick vital records, but that of his wife is not. This April list of the poor contains the additional information that

"Ceasar Ferrits wife Moved to Bostons Janu^r 23. 1795," "Feb^r 1st She moved to Jabez Mans," and "Feb^r 5 Ceasars wife Died."

Sometimes, a town's payment for a poor person's coffin is the only record of his death. In the volume of "Town Orders 1814 to 1841" for Townsend, Massachusetts, there are thirty-two orders for the town to pay for the digging of a grave or the making of a coffin for a deceased pauper, giving the names of the deceased, not all of which appear in the vital records of Townsend.[132]

The town fathers might move to protect the estate of a man who seemed to be in danger of becoming a town charge. The selectmen of Granby, Connecticut, voted on 10 March 1787 that Bennoni Viets "by Reason of age mismanagement and bad husbandry is Likely to Come to want and be Chargable . . . ." So they appointed Asahel Holcomb to "order and Direct . . . the management of his business and all persons are here by forbid trading or Dealling with him the sd bennoni without Liberty & Consent of his sd over Sear first being obtained . . . ."[133]

William Verbach, overseer of the poor for Derby, Vermont, wrote to the Orleans District probate court on 6 March 1856 "that Francis Martineau . . . by excessive drinking and idleness is so spending wasting and lessening as to expose himself and family to want and suffering, and to expose the said town to charge and expense . . . The said overseer therefore requests that inquistion there of be made and a guardian appointed for said Francis Martineau . . . ."[134]

On 10 December 1787 at a town meeting in Framingham, Massachusetts, it was "voted to choose a committee of three persons to look into the affair of Daniel Winchs family" and "voted to choose a person to inform the Judge of Probate of Daniel Winch &

family circumstances and desire some measure may be taken for his benefit & the town."[135]

Daniel was declared an idler and waster of his estate, and the records then switched to the county level, where a guardianship for Daniel appears. Two of his neighbors, Samuel Frost and John Fisk, were appointed guardians for Daniel and his family. They used Daniel's estate to support the family until 23 January 1806 when they reported to the Judge of Probate "that they have exercised that trust for several years and that said idler's estate has been fully expended for his benefit . . . and that said Winch and his family are now under the care and protection of the overseers of the poor."[136] So now the responsibility of caring for Daniel and his family fell back on the town of Framingham.

We often think of the poor as rather passive and accepting of the actions that the town might take on their behalf, but the following petitions show that a town charge sometimes took an active part in determining his fate. In April 1762 the Selectmen of Plaistow, New Hampshire, received the following petitions:[137]

> A penitent Pettion of John Dow . . . that the Town would help me for I am in Low Surcomstance and John Dow Junr Denies Doing any thing for me for he Says he hath no Reason to Do any Thing no more then any other man forthermore he Shews him Self so King to Tell Hannah Parsons that he will see town pays her for Looking after him.

> A Humble Potition of Henery Heseltine and his Wife . . . that thay would come and help me for Benjamin Dow wont do any thing for me and I am in a suffering Condition and hath Ben so this three month and the s^d Dow wont Come and Recon with me and I would have the Slect men to Recon with the s^d Dow for he has got all my Estate in his hands and I have nothing to help my

self with and I would have the Slect men to tak the Estate out of Dow's hands and Let Such Parsons have it that will Let me have things that is needfull . . . .

And Thomas Graves wrote these three petitions to the selectmen of Southborough, Massachusetts.[138]

[undated]
It is the desire of some people that I should make some preposals to the Town how I can take care of my family longer as they think I Saved the Town some corst last year it is a great trouble to me and a corst to the Town for me to live on hire and move about every year if the Town will give me as much this year as I corst the Town the year before last and let me have what common land they can Spare of the back side of the training field and that yord Mr Este fensd in I will contrive some methord to have me a house their before next winter and if the town [?] me of it is not likely they will git red of me any cheaper then they use to for my famely is larger if the Town will grant me my request this year I will take up with Sixty dollars a year after this year so long as I remain as I be now this from Thomas Grave if the Town dont like this preposal they may make me a preposal next but you must remember that my provision is don and their must be something done quick.

March the 9 1803
I will make one more preposal to the Town that is if the Town will pay Mr Brigham Sixteen Dollars and agree to give me Eight Dollars a month this year and five Dollars a month after this year I will not ask the Town for any more till I am so near Starve to death that their will be no hopes of my recovering for father Bellows promised me last Spring he wood give me a nice house spot and garden and I will have a house their before next winter if the Town will agree to this and if the town go on to hire me a house and put out my children it will corst the Town a good deal

but if I must live in a house with a nother family all my days I am
willing to have them poot out if they can have good places I can
poot out some of my children and it wont corst much if any
thing but if the Town poots them out it will corst them somthing
this from Thomas Graves.

Southborough March 7th 1808
To the inhabitants of the Town of Southborugh Greeting,
Gentlemen,
You will doubtless recollect, that when I first came under your
care, the method of supporting me, & my family, was to sell us at
Auction; the cost was then large. Six years ago I inform'd the
Town, that if they would grant me one half the sum, it then cost
them, annually, I would support myself, & family which
remained with me. My request was then granted, & has remain'd
so since. For which grant I render my most sincere thanks.

Gentlemen
I ask your attention to this one petition more, which, if granted,
may be another great saving to the Town. Which is as follows
The house, where I now live, is very convinient for me, & the
owner, Dea Josiah Newton, offers to sell it, I think on very
reasonable terms. If the Town will grant a sum of money, &
purchase the house, & land enough to keep one cow; & let me
have the whole improvement of it during life, I will not be any
other cost to the Town. That is, I wish to have the Town
purchase the house & land, & keep it in their hands, only let me
have the improvement of it. The interest, of what the house &
land will cost, will amount to but one half what I & my family
now cost the Town annually, or one fourth what we once cost
them. Those, who are acquainted with me, will recollect, that I
can use but one hand, & must of consequence be a Town-cost; &
I wish you to call to mind, that it was not through idelness or
intemperance, that I came to want; but it is because the

Providence, of God, has brought me to be a cripple. Seriously consider these things & remember to Do as you would be done by. This is the sincere Petition of your obedient & humble servant Thomas Graves.

The published Southborough vital records show that Thomas Graves died at age 72 years on 26 November 1843. The record adds "Infirmaty-palsied for 30 years on one side. Cooper. He used to sit and work with one hand."[139]

Apprenticeship bonds were sometimes by-products of families falling on hard times. From 1734 to 1805 the city of Boston, Massachusetts, bound out as apprentices 1,100 children to families throughout Massachusetts and Maine.[140] A parent unable to care for his whole family might ask the selectmen or town council to bind out some of his children, and this would be done and recorded in the town records. Occasionally the council or selectmen themselves took the initiative in binding out children, sometimes at a very young age. On 24 December 1793:[141]

Where as it is Enjoyed in the laws of the common Wealth of Massachusetts that the Selectmen do bind out certain persons in certain cases Especially minors we the Subscribers being applyed to as Selectmen of the Town of Ashby . . . by the Widow Susanna Jones . . . to provide for and take care of a child of hers by the name of Polly Tuttle being one year and three days old . . . do put and bind out Polly . . . to . . . Joseph Eaton and his wife to dwell with and serve them from this day until the said Polly shall arive to the full age of Eighton years unless sooner married during all which time the said Apprentice her master and mistress faithfully shall serve in their lawfull commands and their secrets keep she shall do no dammage to her said master nor see it done by others without giving notice thereof to the said master she shall not waste her said masters goods nor lend them unlawfully to others she shall not abcent herself from her Masters House or cervice by day or night without leave but in all things behave her self as a faithfull Apprintice ought to do during the said time and the said Master shall use his utmost Endeavers to teach or cause her to be taught the art of Spinning & Nitting and common House work and provide for her the said Apprintice sufficient meat & drink apparal washings & lodging fitting for an Apprentice during the said time and also suteble Nursing & Doctring during the said time also to teach her to read in the English Bible and Write a ledgable hand if capable & at the Expiration of said time to furnish said Apprintice with two suits of apparal one Sutible for holy day . . . .

Usually children were bound out to local people or nearby relatives, but one example has been found of sending children much further. On 23 May 1882 in Hersey, Maine, the three children of William A. and Ella J. Rhoads, deceased, were bound out. Their son, Lewis W., born 18 July 1875, was bound to John Sargent of Mont Chase, Maine, while their two daughters, Cora Ella, born 17 April 1871, and Abbie P., born 20 February 1873, were bound out to Robert Smart of Brooklin County, Minnesota. Robert Smart may have been a relative of the Rhoads, but if he was, it is not mentioned in the town record.[142]

In 1785, Mr. John Corey applied to the Hopkinton, Rhode Island, Town Council[143] for:

. . . cloathing to fit himself to go to Oblong & WhiteCreek [in New York] . . . and whereas he hath sons (viz) Joshua Cory & Wanton Cory who are able bodied persons to labour & furnish their Father with a decent living . . . it is hereby voted that Mr. John Brown be guardian to the said Wanton Corey . . . that any net proceeds from his labour clear of his support . . . be applyed to the support of his Father.

It was noted also that Mr. Corey had a daughter, Hannah, of about 11 or 12 years of age, and the council voted that she be bound out to Dr. John Auldridge "or any other suitable person till she shall arrive to 18 years of age on the best terms he can for the advantage of the girl & the town."

In the nineteenth century many New England towns established poorhouses or poor farms. Bellingham, Massachusetts, established a poorhouse in 1831 and the first volume of records covers the next twenty years.[144] Each year the names of the inhabitants were reported, along with the expenses of caring for them; also recorded were the monies earned by the poorhouse on produce grown and sold. On 3 March 1834 it was reported that Amey Hill, wife of Jonathan Hill of the state of Ohio, was in the poorhouse and had been there nearly one month. The overseers of the poor had paid the town of Barre, Massachusetts, for Amey's support and her transportation to Bellingham, indicating that Bellingham recognized Amey as an inhabitant and had accepted the responsibility of her care. On 28 February 1835 the birth of Amey's child is recorded and on 3 July 1835 its death; Jedadiah Phipps was paid for making the coffin. Amey continued to live at the poorhouse another twelve years until Dr. Ides agreed to take her in for $1.25 per week.

On 7 October 1843 it was recorded in these records that Sarah Ann Adams had a child born at the poorhouse. A few months later, on 10 July 1844, Sarah, "a poor girl," was let out to Noah J. Arnold until she arrived at the age of eighteen. On 20 July 1847 Noah Arnold was discharged of his care for Sarah because she had turned eighteen, indicating that she had been only fourteen when her baby was born in 1843. The 20th of July may not have been Sarah's exact birthdate, but it would certainly be close to it.

Most of the residents of the poorhouse were elderly—in fact, Abijah Howard contracted with the poorhouse to keep his mother-in-law, Mrs. Gould, for several years. It is not surprising that there are many deaths recorded in the Bellingham volume. A comparison with the Bellingham vital records as published shows that the deaths were recorded there, but generally the date of death was given as a day or two later than in the poorhouse book. The reference for these deaths in the published vital records was a doctor's account book and it appears that the doctor did not always record the death on the day it took place.

At the very back of this Bellingham volume it was noted that William Eccles and his wife, Mary, and child, William, had made application for assistance. William was aged 34 and born in Blackburn, England, his wife was aged 30 and born in Micheltown, Ireland, and their two-year-old son born in Frankford [state or country not given]. They came to Massachusetts on 11 July 1848 and first lived in Lawrence. While at the poorhouse in Bellingham, William and Mary had twins born on 24 November 1848; the births of these twins is not recorded in the published vital records. William and his family left town on 7 February 1849.

By the early 19th century, the overseers of the poor were carrying on extensive correspondence between towns. Many copy books of such correspondence survive and can show the great lengths to which the overseers went to determine the legal settlement of a poor person. Fall River, Massachusetts, has a volume of copies of the letters sent out by the selectmen.[145] They had received a letter from the Overseers of the Poor for the town of Attleborough concerning Juliet G. Davis, believed by Attleborough to be a legal inhabitant of Fall River. The Fall River selectmen wrote back on 3 April 1835:

> You state that Julia [*sic*] G. Davis with her infant child, inhabitants of this town, are in Attleboro and chargable . . . In your postscript, you request us, should you be misinformed in regard . . . to the said Juliet and we in possession of the facts, to give you the necessary information . . . [she] has no settlement in the town of Fall River . . . We learn from the Grandparents of the said Juliet, now living in Westport, that she the said Juliet, is herself an illegitimate - that she was born in Tiverton in the state of Rhode Island - that her mother afterwards married a man by the name of Lapham who was then living in Cumberland R. Island - that immediately after their marriage the said Lapham, with his wife and her child . . . removed to Wareham in the County of Plymouth, where they continued to live about seven or eight years, until the mother of the said Juliet died - and where the said Lapham now live.
>
> We are induced to believe from the above facts, that the said Juliet most probably has a settlement in Wareham - If not she must belong to Rhode Island.

Chapter Sixteen

Church Records

As was noted above, in New England towns, except for Rhode Island, one can find information in the town records about the town churches. Earlier, the pew deeds in the town of Fall River, Massachusetts, were mentioned. Sales of pews were common in the chattel mortgage books. In the town of Richmond, Massachusetts, there are drawn layouts of the meetinghouse several years apart showing where each person or family was to sit. The nearer to the pulpit a family was seated, the higher its social rank in town. On 20 February 1694/5 a committee was chosen to "order and give liberty to make seats for the best advantage and to seate persons" in the meetinghouse of Reading, Massachusetts.[146] It was probably not an easy assignment to rank your neighbors!

In Ipswich, Massachusetts, in 1702 John Curtaine agreed "That he will Carefully Sweep the meeting house & brush down ye seats & Ring ye Bell for Sabbath & Lecture meetings . . . And see y^t all doors & windows be shut Seasonably & take Care of the Bason & Napkin & put up Every day it is to be used the pulpit Cushin & when the Snow is Deep to Shovell paths about ye Doors . . . ." For this service he was to be paid 6 pounds and 10 shillings in grain. Curtaine also agreed to "dig & Cover what Graves shall be needed" at 4 shillings for grown persons and 2 shillings 6 pence for children.[147]

On 4 February 1745/6 in Groton West Parish of Pepperell, Massachusetts, the town records note the descriptions of the "Pews in the Publick meeting house in s^d Parish to the men that are highest in pay in the three Last Rates in s^d Parish on Estates in the following manner" (these are the first three descriptions):[148]

To Richard Warner on the North side of s^d house the Second from the Pulpit on the East side of the same Lieth six feet & three inches on the front and as much on s^d wall and the Debth five feet and three inches to the alley.

2nd To Ebenezer Gillson on the North side of the house ye second from the Pulpit to the west which Lieth four feet and ten inches on ye front and as much on ye wall and the Debth from the wall to the alley is five feet and three Inches.

3rd To Sam^ll Shattuck J^r at ye East end of the house North of ye end Door which Lieth from ye Door on ye front of ye Pew six feet & two inches and as much on the Wall and five feet from the Wall to ye alley.

After laying out thirteen new pews in the meetinghouse in May of 1728, the town committee for Medford, Massachusetts, instructed the new owners that "Theay that have These pews not to Sell Them nor any one of Them To any person or persons Living out of the Town of Medford."[149] Pews could be passed down in a family and are sometimes found mentioned in wills or included in probate inventories.

In Ashby, Massachusetts, there is a "List of persons who filed, previous to March 1st 1829, a request to become members of the Congregational Society in Ashby with the Town Clerk." It included eleven names. At the bottom of the page was a "List of those who have filed certificate as above that they are members of other than said Congregational Society," containing nine names. Unfortunately, it was not indicated to what church they belonged.[150] Later, in October 1831, there is another list, of "those

:Old Church
New·Castle :

persons who have left the first Parish by lodging a Certificate with the Town Clerk." Several names are marked as "Dead," "Removed," or "Returned."[151] In the first volume of town records, one finds that the town clerk copied the above mentioned certificates into the town book. Here are two examples:[152]

> I hereby certify that Stephen Gibson haste become a member of and united in religious worship with the first Baptist society in Ashby and Fitchburg. George Wood, Clerk of said Society. 6 February 1816.

> This may certify that Ebenezer Wythe is a member of the Methodist Society in Ashburnham and pays to their support. 3 April 1816.

In Marlborough, Connecticut, there are similar entries called "Certificates of Dissent from the Congregational Society:"[153]

> September 20th 1817 Joseph Tilden certified that he belonged to the Episcopal Church in Marlborough.

> December 4th Edward Root certified that he belonged to the Methodist Episcopal Society.

Since the towns of New England, except Rhode Island, collected taxes to support the ministers and churches, it was important to know to which church each inhabitant belonged, so that the taxes could be collected and distributed correctly. In Pelham, New Hampshire, on 16 June 1787, seventeen men signed a petition to join the New Parish; additional names were added to the list in 1789, 1790, 1791, and 1792.[154] In March 1844 the treasurer of North Salem, Maine, listed payments to the treasurers of the various churches in town. They included the Congregational Society, the Freewill Baptist Society, the Methodist Society, the Universalist Society, and the Baptist Society. It is interesting that the same man,

Willison Clark, was treasurer of both the Congregational and the Freewill Baptist societies.[155]

In Craftsbury, Vermont, the elders of the Methodist Episcopal Church had their "credentials" recorded in the town book. On 12 April 1820 the town clerk copied the following:[156]

> Know all men by these presents that I, Robert R. Roberts, one of the Bishops of the Methodist Episcopal church, in America, under the protection of Almighty God, and with a single eye to his glory, by the imposition of my hands, and prayer (being assisted by the elders present) have this day set apart, Josiah A. Scarritt for the office of an elder, in the Methodist Episcopal Church; a man whom I judge to be well qualified for the work; And I do hereby recommend him to all, to whom it may concern, as a proper person to administer the sacraments and ordinances; and to feed the flock of Christ, so long as his spirit and practice are such as become the gospel of Christ . . . sixth day of June [1819].

Westmoreland, New Hampshire, on 7 July 1783 "Voted that it is the sence and Opinion of this town that no Shaking Quaker who is not an Inhabitant of this town be allowed to stay in town any more than one night at one time." This record probably refers to the Shakers.[157]

Chapter Seventeen

Town Reports

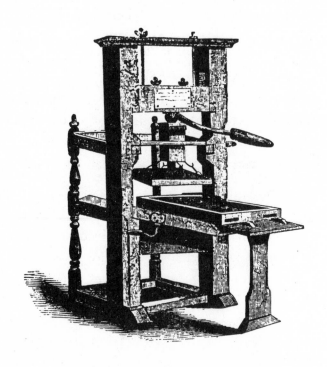

In the nineteenth century many New England towns published annual town reports, including lists of officers and committee members, financial statements, school reports, and reports from the overseers of the poor. Most town reports listed deaths, marriages, and sometimes births, that took place in the preceding year. The local public library is a good place to look for these town reports.

In 1864, Abington, Massachusetts, published *The Selectmen's First Printed Report of the Receipts and Expenditures of the Town of Abington From March 7, 1845, to February 26, 1846.* Expenses for four people at the almshouse were noted, as was a list of payments for "Poor out of the Almes-house, 1845-6," which included the names of the poor and those paid to support them. Payments were made to Jacob Pool for his mother's support from 23 February 1846 to her death, for Isaac Pool and Charles Clinton in their last sicknesses, and for a coffin for Mrs. Erskine.

In 1849, Abington's report begins to list deaths; in 1851, marriages. In 1854 the report notes the names of inmates at the almshouse, and their dates of admission. The 1876 town report for South Abington records the names of those who received aid from the Overseers of the Poor, of students who were not absent or tardy the preceding year, and of high school graduates. The 1887 town report for Hudson, New Hampshire, gives the names of the poor and their caretakers, informs us that a grave was being dug for D.P. Corliss, chronicles births, marriages, and deaths, and acknowledges the students who were not absent or tardy.[158]

Chapter Eighteen

Inquests

Inquests, which in Massachusetts, Maine, and New Hampshire fell under the jurisdiction of the county courts, can be found in the early town records of Rhode Island. "The Early Records of the Town of Warwick" relate that when "Mary Samon daughter of John & Ann Samon aged 9 yeers or ther about" was found drowned, Capt. John Greene and a jury of twelve men heard evidence of Thomas Scranton, aged 25, that

> on ye 18th of february 1665 three hours within Night John Read fatherin-law [i.e. step-father] to Mary Sammon came to Mr. Anthony Loes house to desire hime . . . to light hime . . . with a lanthorne candle, to seeke for his daughterinlaw Mary Samon who was sent to fetch water at y^e brooke & came not againe . . . .

It was decided that the girl,

> eyght or nyne yeers of age was sent by her mother in a very darke nyght alone to a brooke . . . to fetch water & . . . drowned.[159]

Chapter Nineteen

Adoptions

Maine passed its first adoption law in 1855, but both before and after that date, adoptions are found in the town records of Saco:[160]

> Malvina Danforth daughter of Samuel S. Roberts and Amanda M. Roberts - Born in Law - Aug. 29. 1854. and adopted by said Moses and Lavina Oct. 26. 1854. by the following deed of Adoption.

> Deed of Adoption of Malvina
> Amanda Roberts to Moses and Lavina Danforth - Whereas Samuel S. Roberts, and Amanda M. Roberts his wife, were lawfully Married on the Nineteenth day of June A.D. 1854, and about two weeks thereafter the said Samuel S. Roberts absconded and left his Wife . . . without any fault on her part, and without her consent, and she has never heard from him since, that on the twenty ninth day of August A.D. 1854, she became the Mother of a female child, of which the said Samuel S. Roberts, her husband was the father, that the said child is now living, but has never been christened - that the said Amanda is dependent upon her own labor for support, and therefore is able to secure but limited advantages to her child in future; that the present residence of the said Samuel S. Roberts, is unknown . . . that the said Amanda and her said Child are at present living in the town of Saco . . . that she the said Amanda is willing and desirious to make any sacrafice to secure to said child a better home and better advantages . . . And whereas Moses Danforth and Lavina Danforth his wife are willing and desirous to receive said Child from the said Amanda, as their own to give to it their own name, and to secure to it all the advantages and benefits which one of their own natural offspring would have or be entitled to,

Therefore - Be it known - That I the said Amanda Roberts, the natural mother and acting guardian of said child, in consideration of premises, do hereby willingly and of my own accord, give and convey said Child unto the said Moses and Lavinia, to hold as their own forever hereafter hereby giving and releasing unto the said Moses and Lavina, with said Child, all the rights and powers, both natural and legal, which I as Mother ever had, or now have to, or over said Child. And we the said Moses and Lavina, hereby adopt said Child from the said Amanda as our own, and Christen it Malvina Danforth - And we hereby give, Grant, guarantee and secure unto the said Malvina, all the care, rights, benefits and privileges of our home and estate, the same as if she were our own natural offspring, and to be unto her and she unto us, as a Father, Mother and Child forever hereafter.

In Witness Whereof, the parties have hereunto set their hands and seals this twenty sixth day of October A.D. 1854.

A few years later, the Saco records show another adoption:

Deed of Adoption
Know all men by these Presents that whereas I Joseph H. Foss have jointly with Jane my wife both of Saco . . . this day signed a petition to the Judge of Probate for said County for leave to adopt as our child Bessie Ella Chamberlin the child of Charlotte Chamberlin of Biddeford . . . and to have it assume the name of Bessie Ella Foss; and whereas the said Charlotte Chamberlin has this day signed her written consent to the adoption of said Child and its change of name and has requested the Judge of Probate to make the necessary decree;

Now therefore in consideration thereof, and in consideration that she Bessie Ella Chamberlin otherwise known as Bessie Ella Foss shall remain with us as a child and not permanently leave us until she arrives at twenty one years of age (21) or until she marries - provided we live until she arrives to be twenty one (21) years of age.

Now it is understood also that she is not to be debarred from her rights under this instrument if she is caused not of her own free will whether by unsuitable treatment, care, or provision or otherwise from us or any of my family, to leave us before she arrives at twenty one years of age.

Now therefore I agree to give and promise to pay her Bessie Ella Chamberlin otherwise known as Bessie Ella Foss the sume of one hundred (100) dollars when she becomes twenty one (21) years of age, also in case she married before she arrives to be twenty one years of age, I also promise and agree to give and furnish her with a marriage outfit worth not less than one hundred and fifty (150) dollars. I also promise and agree to provide her a home, and good and suitable board and good and suitable clothing and to give her a good ordinary District School education, and to provide and care for her in Sickness and health and treat her as I could an own child - and at my decease she is to be provided for as above from my property as though I had lived.

Witness my hand and seal at said Saco this sixteenth day of November A.D. 1863.

Summary

Even though the kinds of things to be found in town records are much the same all over New England, there are a few significant differences which must be noted. In Rhode Island the town records include both probate and land records, which in Massachusetts and the states which grew out of it (Maine and New Hampshire) have always been kept on the county level. In Connecticut and Vermont, the land records are kept by the towns; Vermont was heavily settled by Rhode Island and Connecticut people. In both of these states, however, probates are recorded in districts which may include several towns. These probate districts often have the same names as the counties, but the district and county boundary lines are not always identical.

In Rhode Island, Connecticut, and Vermont, therefore, the genealogist will be able to accomplish far more research on the town level than in the other three New England states, because more types of records will likely be grouped in one place. Furthermore, in these states, town clerks often doubled as recorders of deeds, and used their intimate knowledge of their neighbors to add important details to the official record. For instance, when preparing the index in front of each deed book, some town clerks noted filial or fraternal relationships not indicated in the deeds themselves. Where these early indexes have survived, they are often of real value.

A historian or genealogist who delves into town records is not likely to be disappointed. Even if the unlikely occurs and no mention is found of the person sought, the researcher cannot help but acquire a fresh picture of the life and interests of the people of that period and place. The knowledge gained will be valuable in future work and will enable him, or her, to approach the records of the next town with more confidence.

Endnotes

1. John C. Reilly, "Gloucester (Mass.) Apprenticeship Papers," *The Essex Genealogist*, 14 [1994]:80-85; 138-142; 199-204.

2. Josiah Henry Benton, *Warning Out in New England, 1656-1817* (Boston, 1911; reprint Heritage Books, 1992), p. 10.

3. Nathaniel B. Shurtleff, ed., *Records of the Governor and Company of the Massachusetts Bay in New England* (Boston, 1853), 1:117, 161.

4. *Ibid.*, 2:197, 208.

5. *Ibid.*, 4, part 1:336.

6. Benton, *Warning Out in New England*, pp. 63-64, 78.

7. Lebanon [Connecticut], "Town Records," 1:36.

8. Benton, *Warning Out in New England*, p. 108.

9. *Ibid.*, p. 100.

10. *Ibid.*, p. 90.

11. Claremont [New Hampshire], "Town Records," 1:236.

12. Jane Fletcher Fiske, "Rhode Island Men Made Freemen 1760 to 1762," *Rhode Island Roots*, 10[1984]:81-82; 11[1985]:7, 17-19, 43-47, 73-76; 12[1986]:10-11, 33-36, 79-86.

13. Reading, Massachusetts, "Records Town Meeting 1648-1738," microfilm in *Early Massachusetts Records, Inc.*, [hereafter *EMR*], Reel 1, Target 1, p. 135.

14. J. Hammond Trumbull, *The Public Records of the Colony of Connecticut* (Hartford, 1850), p. 551.

15. *Watertown Records* (Watertown, 1894), 1:1.

16. Allen Soule, ed., *Laws of Vermont, State Papers of Vermont* (Montpelier, 1964), 12:84.

17. Bruce C. Daniels, *The Connecticut Town, Growth and Development, 1635-1790* (Middletown, 1979), p. 68.

18. *Ibid.*, p. 69.

19. *Ibid.*, p. 70; *Town Government in Massachusetts*, p. 39.

20. Northwood [New Hampshire], "Town Records," 1:186.

21. Ann S. Lainhart, "The Descendants of Abraham Bryant of Reading," *The New England Historical and Genealogical Register*, 137 [1983]:235-259, 317-339.

22. Ipswich [Massachusetts], "Town Meetings, 1720-1738," p. 8.

23. Samuel Freeman, Esq., *The Town Officer; or the Power and Duty of*

Endnotes

Selectmen, Town Clerks, Town Treasurers, Overseers of the Poor, Assessors, Constables, Collectors of Taxes, Surveyors of High Ways, Surveyors of Lumber, Fence Viewers, and other Town Officers as Contained in the Laws of the Commonwealth of Massachusetts ... (Boston, 1793).

24. Unity [New Hampshire], "Town Records," p. 305.

25. John Fairfield Sly, Town Government in Massachusetts (1620-1930), (Cambridge, 1930), p. 45.

26. Simsbury, Connecticut, "Vital Records, Birth, Death, Marriage, Book 3," flyleaf.

27. David Pulsifer, "Transcript of Roxbury [Massachusetts] Town Records, Vol. 1, 1648-1730/1," p. 12.

28. "Records, Town of Hull [Massachusetts], 1657-1841," pp. 220-222.

29. Woburn [Massachusetts], "Town Records Vol. 3 [Selectmen, Land, Assessor 1680-1693]," EMR, Reel 1, Target 3, p. 129.

30. Woburn, Massachusetts, "Town Records Vol. 4 [miscellany 1693-1711]," EMR, Reel 1, Target 4, p. 152.

31. Ipswich [Massachusetts], "Town Meetings, 1697-1719," p. 70.

32. Zara Jones Powers, ed., New Haven [Connecticut] Town Records, 1684-1769 [Ancient Town Records], (New Haven, 1962), 3:278.

33. Cape Elizabeth [Maine], "Town Records, 1724-1823," p. 103.

34. Powers, New Haven [Connecticut] Town Records, 3:567.

35. Simsbury, Connecticut, "Vital Records, Birth, Death, Marriage, Book 3," p. 57.

36. Deerfield, Massachusetts, "Town Book to 1762," p. 158.

37. Unity [New Hampshire] "Town Records," p. 261.

38. Mark Williams, Granby [Connecticut] Town Records (Granby, 1986), p. 4.

39. New Braintree [Massachusetts], "Town Records, Vol. 2, 1749-1799," p. 315.

40. Rutland County, Vermont, "Miscellaneous Record, Chittenden [Philadelphia]," p. 24.

41. Deerfield, Massachusetts, "Town Book to 1762," p. 106.

42. Marlborough, Connecticut, "Vital Records Birth, Death, Marriage," pp. 203-204.

43. Simsbury, Connecticut, "Vital Records Birth, Death, Marriage," Book 1, p. 112.

44. Barnstable [Massachusetts], "Town Records," (mss. at the New England

Historic Genealogical Society, Boston), 1:22.

45. Chichester [New Hampshire], "Town Records, Vol. 1, 1727-1800," p. 57.

46. Hatfield [Massachusetts], "Records, 1702-1740," p. 53.

47. Bernardston [Massachusetts], "Town Meetings, 1762-1815," (mss. in the Corbin Collection at the New England Historic Genealogical Society, Boston), p. 119.

48. Natick, Massachusetts, "Indian Records 1700-1773," *EMR*, Reel 2, Target 6.

49. Ipswich [Massachusetts], "Town Meetings 1720-1738," p. 96.

50. Unity, New Hampshire, "Town Records," p. 605.

51. Sherborn, Massachusetts, "Envelope No. 12 [Assessor, Land, Military, Church 1730-1900]," *EMR*, Reel 3, Target 15.

52. Croyden [New Hampshire], "Town Records, Vol. 1," p. 232.

53. Powers, *New Haven Town Records*, 3:173.

54. Natick, Massachusetts, "Misc. Book 13," *EMR*, Reel 1, Target 4, p. 26.

55. Billerica, Massachusetts, "Vol. 5 1780-1792 [Treasurer 1779-1792]," *EMR*, Reel 2, Target 5, p. 278.

56. Lincoln, Massachusetts, "1758 [Treasurer 1758-1788]," *EMR*, Reel 4, Target 38.

57. Newton, Massachusetts, "Receipts to Treasurer 1764 to 1767 [1764-1778]," *EMR*, Reel 2, Target 9, no pagination.

58. Bettye Hobbs Pruitt, *The Massachusetts Tax Valuation List of 1771* (Boston, 1978).

59. Dracut, Massachusetts, "Real Estate Valuation 1820 to 1829," *EMR*, Reel 6, Target 22, no pagination.

60. Reading [Massachusetts], "Town Meeting 1648-1738," *EMR*, Reel 1, Target 1, p. 79.

61. Heath, Massachusetts, "Town Records, 1785-1848," p. 169.

62. Priscilla Hammond, "The Town Book of Bow, New Hampshire," (typescript at the New England Historic Genealogical Society, Boston), p. 91.

63. *A Report of the Record Commissioners of the City of Boston, Containing the Records of the Boston Selectmen, 1716 to 1736* (Boston, 1885), p. 56.

64. Derby [Vermont], "Town Records, Deeds, Vol. 5, 1827-1859," p. 88.

65. "Book of Records in the Precinct of Lincoln [Massachusetts] from 1746-

1810," *EMR*, Reel 4, Target 36, no pagination.

66. Marlborough, Connecticut, "Vital Records, Birth, Death, Marriage," p. 141-2.

67. "The Town Records of (No.) Salem, Franklin Co., Maine," Book 6, no pagination.

68. Gloucester, Massachusetts, Archives, 1867, Doc. #91.

69. Reading, Massachusetts, "Records Town Meeting 1648-1738," *EMR*, Reel 1, Target 1, p. 172.

70. "No. 1, Dexter Town Book," p. 134-5.

71. Ruth Wilder Sherman, "Early Bristol RI Ear Marks and Horse Descriptions," *The American Genealogist*, 63 [1988]: 247-248; 64 [1989]: 53-54, 120, 183-184, 247-248; 65 [1990]: 54-55, 118-119, 184, 248. See also Margery I. Matthews, "Earmarks Registered in Foster [Rhode Island], 1788-1852," *Rhode Island Roots*, 16 [1990]:79-87, 112-117; Margery I. Matthews, "Earmarks Registered in Scituate [Rhode Island]," *Rhode Island Roots*, 17 [1991]:9-15, 46-50, 91-93.

72. *Early Records of the Town of Portsmouth [Rhode Island]* (Providence, 1901), p. 278.

73. Deerfield, Massachusetts, "Town Records 1763-1794," at end of volume, no pagination.

74. Dr. Thomas H. Roderick, "Genealogical Evidence: Marks for Cattle and Sheep," *National Genealogical Society Quarterly*, 57 [1969]:88-92.

75. Ipswich [Massachusetts], "Town Meetings, 1697-1719," p. 46.

76. Marlborough, Connecticut, "Vital Records Birth, Death, Marriage," p. 182.

77. Suffield, Connecticut, "Vital Records, Birth, Death, Marriage," p. 152.

78. "Nantucket Proprietors Records, 1716-1808."

79. "Reading [Strays, Cattle register, Slave 1753-1788]," *EMR*, Reel 5, Target 24, no pagination.

80. Croyden [New Hampshire], "Town Records, Vol. 1," p. 263.

81. Suffield, Connecticut, "Vital Records Birth, Death, Marriage," p. 143.

82. Simsbury, Connecticut, "Vital Records, Birth, Death, Marriage," Book 3, p. 4. East Hartford [Connecticut], "Birth, Death, Marriage Record," no pagination.

83. Mark Williams, *Granby* [Connecticut] *Town Records* (Granby, 1986), p. 57.

84. East Hartford [Connecticut], "Birth, Death, Marriage Record," no

pagination.

85. Jean C. Stutz, *South Kingstown, Rhode Island, Town Council Records, 1771-1795* (1988), pp. 217, 304.

86. "Chattell Mortgage Book 1836-1839, Lynn, Massachusetts," (Essex County Collection, Phillips Library, Peabody Essex Museum, Salem, Massachusetts).

87. Burlington Book of Records No. 2 [1825-1856], *EMR*, Roll 1, Target 2, p. 196.

88. Hersey [Maine], "Town Records," 1:11.

89. Gorham, Maine, "Vol. 1 1839-61, Miscellaneous Records," p. 17.

90. Ibid., 1:54.

91. Ibid., 1:36.

92. Hatfield [Massachusetts], "Records, 1702-1740," p. 20.

93. Reading [Massachusetts], "Town Meeting 1648-1738," *EMR*, Reel 1, Target 1, p. 113.

94. Hatfield [Massachusetts], "Records, 1702-1740," p. 138.

95. Croyden [New Hampshire], "Town Records, Vol. 1," p. 11.

96. Montville [Maine], "Town Records, 1765-1826," p. 80.

97. "Records of the Town of Woodstock [Maine], Book 1," p. 26-27.

98. Derby [Vermont], "Town Records, Deeds, Vol. 5, 1827-1859," p. 122.

99. Groton, Massachusetts, "Papers Relating to the Revolution . . . Papers Relating to Shays' Rebellion," *EMR*, Reel 4, Target 18, loose papers not numbered.

100. Sherborn, Massachusetts, "Envelope No. 1 [Assessor, Land, Church warrants, Military, Cemetery 1703-1878]," *EMR*, Reel 3, Target 14, loose papers not numbered.

101. "The Book of the Treasurer's Accompts in Lincoln [Massachusetts] 1755," *EMR*, Reel 4, Target 38, no pagination.

102. Reading, Massachusetts, "Orders, Receipts 1776-1810 [Selectmen, Orders, Treasurer]," *EMR*, Reel 2, Target 6, pp. 31, 32, 33.

103. Acton, Massachusetts, "Town Meeting Records Vol. 3 1819-1839," *EMR*, Reel 1, Target 3, no pagination.

104. Ashby, Massachusetts, "[Miscellaneous papers, petitions, taxes, school 1777-1833]," *EMR*, Reel 5, Target 21, loose papers not numbered.

105. New Braintree [Massachusetts], "Town Records, Vol. 2, 1749-1799," p. 74.

106. Hinsdale [New Hampshire], "Town Records, Vol. 1," p. 47.

107. Groton, Massachusetts, "Papers Relating to the Revolution . . . Papers Relating to Shays' Rebellion," *EMR*, Reel 4, Target 18, loose papers not numbered.

108. New Braintree [Massachusetts], "Town Records, Vol. 2, 1749-1799," p. 187.

109. Cary, Maine, "Vital Records, Vol. 1," p. 77.

110. Dighton, Massachusetts, "Rebellion Record, Volume 1, 1863," pp. 22, 24, 26, 32, 44.

111. Ipswich [Massachusetts], "Town Meetings, 1720-1738," p. 172.

112. Acton, Massachusetts, "Town Meeting Records Vol. 3 1819-1839," *EMR*, Reel 1, Target 3, no pagination.

113. Salem [New Hampshire], "Town Records," 3:15.

114. Andover, Vermont, "Town Records, Vol. 2," p. 108.

115. Ann S. Lainhart, "Weston Cautions 1757 to 1803," *The New England Historical and Genealogical Register*, 144 [1990]:215-224.

116. Natick, Massachusetts, "Misc. Book 13 [Treasurer, Perambulations 1774-1839]," *EMR*, Reel 1, Target 4, p. 25.

117. Ann S. Lainhart, "Cambridge, Massachusetts, Notifications and Warnings Out (1788-1797)," *The New England Historical and Genealogical Register*, 146 [1992]:77-90.

118. Woburn, Massachusetts, "Records Vol. 1 [Miscellany 1640-1742]," *EMR*, Reel 1, Target 1, p. 74.

119. Woburn, Massachusetts, "Town Records Vol. 4 [Miscellany 1693-1711]," *EMR*, Reel 1, Target 4, pp. 125-127.

120. "Cumberland Town Council Records," 7:53.

121. Jean C. Stutz, *South Kingston, Rhode Island, Town Council Records, 1771-1795*, (1988), pp. 329, 330.

122. Athol, Massachusetts, "Town Records 1737-1792, Vol. 1," p. 88.

123. Reading, Massachusetts, "Orders, Receipts 1776-1810," *EMR*, Reel 2, Target 6, p. 3.

124. Simsbury, Connecticut, "Vital Records, Birth, Death, Marriage, Book 3," p. 17.

125. Henry C. Hallowell, *Vital Records of Townsend, Massachusetts* (Boston, 1992), p. 462.

126. Ashby, Massachusetts, "Selectmen's Records 1828-1857," *EMR*, Reel 2,

Target 7, no pagination.

127. Brooksville, Maine, "Town Records," (typescript at the New England Historic Genealogical Society, Boston), p. 234.

128. Rutland County, Vermont, "Miscellaneous Record, Chittenden [Philadelphia]," p. 81.

129. Natick, Massachusetts, "Misc. Book 13," *EMR*, Reel 1, Target 4, p. 33.

130. Harriet Russell Stratton, *A Book of Strattons* (New York, 1918), 1:178, 2:31.

131. Townsend [Massachusetts], "Pauper Book," *EMR*, Reel 2, Target 9, pp. 58, 60.

132. Natick, Massachusetts, "Misc. Book 13," *EMR*, Reel 1, Target 4, p. 66.

133. Mark Williams, *Granby [Connecticut] Town Records* (Granby, 1986), p. 6.

134. Derby [Vermont], "Town Records, Deeds, Vol. 5 1827-1859," p. 470.

135. Framingham, Massachusetts, "Miscellany of Town Records 1781-1789," *EMR*, Reel 1, Target 3, no pagination.

136. Middlesex County, Massachusetts, Probate, First Series #25209.

137. Plaistow [New Hampshire], "Town Records," 2:38.

138. Southborough, Massachusetts, "Box 2 — Town Papers Welfare 1736-1840," loose papers.

139. *Vital Records of Southborough, Massachusetts, To the End of the Year 1849* (Worcester, 1903), p. 169.

140. "The Indentures of Boston's Poor Apprentices: 1734-1805," *Publications of The Colonial Society of Massachusetts*, 43 [1966]:417-468.

141. Ashby, Massachusetts, "Overseers of the Poor 1791-1833," *EMR*, Reel 5, Target 22, loose papers not numbered.

142. Hersey [Maine], "Town Records," 2:9.

143. Hopkinton [Rhode Island], "Town Council Records," 5:251.

144. "Records relating to the Poor house, & farm, in Bellingham [Massachusetts]."

145. Fall River, Massachusetts, "Records of Selectmen's Letters 1830-1840," no pagination.

146. Reading, Massachusetts, "Records [of] Town Meeting 1648-1738," *EMR*, Reel 1, Target 1, p. 59.

147. Ipswich [Massachusetts], "Treasurer and Selectmen Records, 1699-1727," no pagination.

148. Pepperell, Massachusetts, "Town Records Vol. 1 [miscellany 1742-1791],"

EMR, Reel 1, Target 1, p. 8.

149. "Records of the Town of Medford [Massachusetts] Vol. 1, 1675-1718," *EMR*, Reel 1, Target 1, p. 216.

150. Ashby, Massachusetts, "[Miscellaneous papers, Petitions, Taxes, School 1777-1833]," *EMR*, Reel 5, Target 21, loose papers not numbered.

151. Ashby, Massachusetts, "Town Records 1795-1821, Marriages 1794-1818 Vol. 2," *EMR*, Reel 1, Target 2, p. 219.

152. Ashby, Massachusetts, "Town Records 1767-1795, Vol. 1," *EMR*, Reel 1, Target 1, pp. 327, 331.

153. Marlborough, Connecticut, "Vital Records Birth, Death, Marriage," p. 240.

154. Pelham [New Hampshire], "Town Records, Vol. 1, 1746-1844," p. 116.

155. "The Town Records of (No.) Salem, Franklin County, Maine," Book 7, no pagination.

156. Craftsbury [Vermont], "Vital Records Index, Vol. 1, 1781-1900," p. 82.

157. Westmoreland [New Hampshire] "Town Records," 1:155.

158. *Annual Reports of the Selectmen, Treasurer and Board of Education of the Town of Hudson [New Hampshire] for the Year ending March 1st, 1887.*

159. *The Early Records of the Town of Warwick*, (Providence, 1926) p. 312.

160. Saco [Maine], "Vital Records, 1840-1880," p. 147.

Appendix A

New England Town Records in Print

CONNECTICUT

Colchester	*Extracts from the Records of Colchester* (Hartford, 1864), covers the period from 1713 to 1730.
Derby	*Town Records of Derby, Connecticut, 1655-1710* (Derby, 1901).
Enfield	*History of Enfield* (Lancaster, Penn. 1900). Volume I includes the "Commoners' Book, Book A, 1711-1808," "Committee Book," and "Land Grants."
Granby	Mark Williams, *Granby Town Records* (Granby, 1986).
Lyme	Jean Chandler Burr, *Lyme Records, 1667-1730* (Stonington, 1968).
New Haven	*New Haven Colony Historical Society: Ancient Town Records, 1649-1769*, 3 volumes (New Haven, 1917, 1919, 1962).
Suffield	H.S. Sheldon, *Documentary History of Suffield . . . 1660-1749* (Springfield, 1879).
Waterbury	K.A. Prichard, *Proprietors' Records of the Town of Waterbury, Connecticut, 1677-1761* (Mattatuck Historical Society, 1911).

MAINE

Augusta	Charles Elventon Nash, *The History of Augusta* (Augusta, 1904), has excerpts of town records and tax lists.
Brooksville	Town Meetings, 1817-1850, Brooksville (1949), typescript at the New England Historic Genealogical Society.
Buxton	Cyrus Woodman, *Records of the Proprietors of Narraganset Township, No. 1, now the Town of Buxton, York County, Maine, 1733-1811* (Concord, N.H., 1871).
Limerick	*Vital Records of Limerick, Maine, with a full copy of Limerick Town Records Book A (1989).*
New Gloucester	J.W. Penny, *Records of the Proprietors of New Gloucester*, Maine Historical Society, Collections (1897), 2nd Series, Vol. VIII:263-288.
Pejepscot	J.P. Baxter, *The Pejepscot Proprietors: Records and Papers to*

1766, *Documentary History of Maine*, XXIV:199-464
(Portland, 1916).

Pemaquid   *Papers relating to Pemaquid* (Albany, 1856). Also in Maine
               Historical Society, Collections, 1st Series, V:1-139.

Standish   Records [Standish]. *Maine Historical and Genealogical
               Recorder*, V:233-239, VI:359-361.

MASSACHUSETTS

Alford   Alford, Massachusetts, Tax Records, 1815-1816, typescript at
               the New England Historic Genealogical Society.

Amherst   J.F. Jameson, *Records of the Town of Amherst,1735-1788*
               (Amherst, 1884).

Andover   Betty Senechal, Andover, Massachusetts, Early Land Grant
               Records, Mostly Prior to 1700, typescript at the New
               England Historic Genealogical Society.

Blandford   Beatrice Bagg Littlefield, Extracts from the Town Records of
               Blandford, Mass., typescript at the New England Historic
               Genealogical Society.

Boston   Boston Record Commissioners' Series.
               Vol. 1 [17th Century tax lists] (1881)
               Vol. 2, Boston Records, 1634-1660, and the Book of
                  Possessions (1881)
               Vol. 5, [miscellaneous records] (1884)
               Vol. 7, Boston Records from 1660 to 1701 (1881)
               Vol. 8, Boston Records from 1700 to 1728 (1883)
               Vol. 10, Miscellaneous Papers (1886)
               Vol. 11, Records of Boston Selectmen, 1701 to 1715 (1884)
               Vol. 12, Boston Records from 1729 to 1742 (1885)
               Vol. 13, Records of Boston Selectmen, 1716 to 1736 (1885)
               Vol. 14, Boston Town Records, 1742 to 1757 (1885)
               Vol. 15, Boston Town Records, 1736 to 1742 (1886)
               Vol. 16, Boston Town Records, 1758 to 1769 (1886)
               Vol. 17, Selectmen's Minutes from 1742-3 to 1753 (1887)
               Vol. 18, Boston Town Records, 1770 through 1777 (1887)
               Vol. 19, Selectmen's Minutes from 1754 through 1763
                  (1887)
               Vol. 20, Selectmen's Minutes from 1764 through 1768
                  (1889)

Vol. 23, Selectmen's Minutes from 1769 through April, 1775 (1893)

Vol. 25, Selectmen's Minutes from 1776 through 1786 (1894)

Vol. 26, Boston Town Records, 1778 to 1783 (1895)

Vol. 27, Selectmen's Minutes from 1789 through 1798 (1896)

Vol. 29, Miscellaneous Papers (1900)

Vol. 31, Boston Town Records, 1784 to 1796 (1903)

Vol. 33, Minutes of the Selectmen's Meetings 1799 to, and including, 1810 (1904)

Vol. 35, Boston Town Records, 1796 to 1813 (1905)

Vol. 37, Boston Town Records, 1814 to 1822 (1906)

Vol. 38, Minutes of the Selectmen's Meetings, 1811 to 1817, and Part of 1818 (1908)

Vol. 39, Minutes of the Selectmen's Meetings from September 1,1818, to April 24, 1822 (1909)

Boxford	Boxford Town Records, 1685-1706. *Essex Institute Historical Collections* (Salem, 1910), 36:41-103.
Braintree	S.A. Bates, *Records of the Town of Braintree, 1640-1793* (Randolph, Mass., 1886).
Bridgewater	*Town Records of Bridgewater, Massachusetts* (Brockton, 1889).
Brookline	*Town Records of Brookline, 1838-1884*, 3 volumes (Brookline, 1888, 1892).
Cambridge	*The Records of the Town of Cambridge, Massachusetts, 1630-1703* (Cambridge, 1901).
	The Register Book of the Lands and Houses in the "New Towne" and the Town of Cambridge (Cambridge, 1896).
Charlestown	Charlestown Land Records, 1638-1802, Boston Record Commissioners' Report, Vol. III, 2nd. Ed. (Boston, 1883).
Concord	*Concord Town Records, 1732-1820* (Concord, 1894).
Dedham	Don Gleason Hill, Julius H. Tuttle, and Benjamin Fisher, *The Early Records of the Town of Dedham, Massachusetts, 1636-1766*, 5 volumes (Dedham, 1892-1968).
	Don Gleason Hill, *The Record of the Town Meetings of Dedham, 1877-1896* (Dedham, 1896).
Dorchester	Dorchester Town Records, 1632-1691, Boston Record Commissioners' Report, Vol. IV, 2nd. ed. (Boston, 1883).
	Tax Payers, Town of Dorchester, 1849-1869 (Boston, 1849-1869).

Dudley	*Town Records of Dudley, Massachusetts, 1732-1794*, 2 volumes (Pawtucket, RI, 1895).
Duxbury	Geo. Netheridge, *Old Records of the Town of Duxbury, Massachusetts, 1642-1770* (Plymouth, 1893).
Fitchburg	W.A. Davis, *The Old Record of the Town of Fitchburg, Massachusetts*, 8 volumes (Fitchburg, 1893).
Groton	S.A. Green, *Early Records of Groton, Massachusetts, 1662-1707* (Groton, 1880).
Haverhill	Haverhill Records, 4 volumes, typescript at the New England Historic Genealogical Society.
Ipswich	G.A. Schefield, *Ancient Records of the Town of Ipswich* (Ipswich, 1899).
Lancaster	*The Early Records of Lancaster, Massachusetts, 1643-1725* (Lancaster, 1884).
Lunenburg	*The Proprietors' Records of the Town of Lunenburg, Massachusetts . . . 1729-1833* (Fitchburg, 1897).
Lynn	*Records of y[e] Towne Meetings of Lynn, 1691-1783*, 7 volumes (Lynn, 1949-1971).
Manchester	*The Commoners' Records in Town Records of Manchester*, 2 volumes (Salem, 1889-1891).
Mendon	*The Proprietors' Records of the Town of Mendon, 1667-1816* (Amherst, 1899).
Milton	*Milton Town Records, 1662-1729* (Milton, 1930).
Nantucket	F.B. Hough, *Papers Relating to the Island of Nantucket* (Albany, 1856).
Oxford	Mary deWitt Freeland, *The Records of Oxford Mass.* (Albany, 1894).
Pelham	Pelham Proprietors' Records, 1738-1743, and Town Records, 1743-1897, *History of Pelham* (Amherst, 1898).
Plymouth	W.T. Davis, *Records of the Town of Plymouth, 1636-1783*, 3 volumes (Plymouth, 1889, 1892, 1903).
Plympton	Charles H. Bricknell, Plympton, Mass., Town and Parish Records, 1695-1835, 7 volumes, typescript at NEHGS.
Rowley	*Rowley: the Early Records of the Town of Rowley, Mass., 1639-1672* (Rowley, 1894).
Roxbury	Roxbury Land Records and Church Records, Boston Record Commissioners' Report, VI, 2nd Ed. (Boston, 1884).
Salem	N.O. Howes, *Salem Town Records, 1634-1691*, 3 volumes.
Springfield	H.R. Burt, *First Century of the History of Springfield: the Official Records, 1636-1736* (Springfield, 1898).

Sudbury	*The War Years in the Town of Sudbury, Massachusetts, 1765-1781* (Sudbury, 1975).
Tisbury	W.S. Swift and J.W. Cleveland, *Records of the Town of Tisbury, Massachusetts, 1669-1864* (Boston, 1903).
Topsfield	*Town Records of Topsfield, Massachusetts*, Vol. I, 1659-1739 (Topsfield, 1917).
Watertown	*Watertown Records*, 8 volumes.
Wenham	*Wenham Town Records, 1642-1776*, 3 volumes (Salem, 1930, 1940).
Weston	M.F. Piere, *Town of Weston: Records of the First Precinct, 1744-1754, and of the Town, 1754-1803* (Boston, 1893). M.F. Piere, *Town of Weston, Records, 1804-1826* (Boston, 1894). *Town of Weston, The Tax Lists, 1757-1827* (Boston, 1897).
Worcester	F.P. Rice, *Early Records of the Town of Worcester, 1722-1783*, volumes 2, 3, and 4, of Worcester Society of Antiquity, Collections.

NEW HAMPSHIRE

Bow	The Town Book of Bow, 1767-1820 (1933), typescript at the New England Historic Genealogical Society. Records of the Proprietors of Bow, 1727-1783 (1933), typescript at the New England Historic Genealogical Society.
Concord	*Concord Town Records, 1732-1820* (Concord, 1894).
Hanover	*Records of the Town of Hanover, New Hampshire, 1761-1818* (Hanover, 1905).
Lebanon	Proprietors' Records of Lebanon, 1761-1774, in *History of Lebanon* (Concord, 1908).
Manchester	G.W. Browne, *Early Records of the Town of Derryfield, Now Manchester, New Hampshire*, 5 volumes.
Mason	A.S. Batchellor, Records of the Meetings of the Masonian Proprietors, 1748-1846, *New Hampshire State Papers*, Vol. XXIX, Pt. 2, 400-644.
Peterborough	The Records of the Original Proprietors of Peterborough, an appendix to *History of the Town of Peterborough* (Boston, 1876).

Appendix A

RHODE ISLAND

Newport
Included in vol. 1 of John Russell Bartlett, ed., *Records of the Colony of Rhode Island and Providence Plantations in New England* (Providence, 1856; reprint ed., New York, 1968).

Portsmouth
Clarence S. Brigham, ed., *Early Records of the Town of Portsmouth, 1639-1697* (Providence, 1901)

Providence
Horatio Rogers, ed. *Early Records of the Town of Providence*, 21 volumes (Providence, 1892-1915)

So. Kingstown
Jean C. Stutz, *South Kingstown, Rhode Island, Town Council Records, 1771-1795* (1988)

Warwick
Howard M. Chapin, ed., *Early Records of the Town of Warwick* (Providence, 1926)

VERMONT

Weybridge
Weybridge Proprietors' Records, 1762-1811, typescript at the New England Historic Genealogical Society.

Some town records, such as Guilford's, are printed in the *Vermont Historical Gazetteer*.

DAR Typescripts
at the New England Historic
Genealogical Society

FOR MASSACHUSETTS TOWNS

Acton, Town Officers, 1775-1783.
Andover, Town Meeting Reports, 1775-1783, Officers.
Attleboro, Town Meeting Reports.
Town Officers of Barnstable, 1775-1783.
Barnstable see Truro
Civil Town Officers, 1775-1783, Bernardston and Northfield.
Beverly, Town Officers, 1775-1783.
Blandford, Town Officers, 1775-1783.
Boxboro's First Officers, 1783.
Bradford, Town Officers, 1775-1783.
Town Officers of Town of Brookline, 1775-1783.
Chelsea, Town Officers, 1774-1783.
Town Officers of Concord.
Dartmouth Town Records.
Douglas, Town Officers, 1775-1783.
Dracut, Town Officers, 1775-1783.
List of Civil Town Officers, 1775-1783, Town of Duxbury.
Town Officials of Eastham (including Orleans).
Fitchburg, Town Officers, 1775-1783.
Grafton, Town Officers, 1775-1783.
Harvard, Town Officers, 1775-1783.
Haverhill, Town Officers, 1775-1783.
Ipswich, Town Officers, 1775-1783.
Lee, Town Officers, 1777-1783.
Leverett, Town Officers, 1775-1783.
Town of Lincoln, Town Officers.
Mansfield, Town Officials Mar. 1775-Dec. 1783.
Marblehead, Town Officers, 1775-1783.

Appendix A

Civil Service During the Revolution, Methuen.

Town of Montgomery, Doings of Town Meetings.

Civilian Service in the American Revolution at Monson.

Nantucket, Town Officers, 1775-1783.

Northfield see Bernardston

Orange, Warwick, Wendell.

Town Officers of Petersham, 1775-1783.

List of Civil Town Officers of the Town of Shutesbury, 1775-1783.

Swansea, Town Officers, 1775-1777-1779.

Tewksbury, Town Officers, 1775-1782.

List of Civil Town Officers of Truro, Wellfleet, and Barnstable.

Uxbridge, Town Officers, 1775-1783.

Warwick see Orange

Watertown, Town Officials, 1775-1783.

Wellfleet see Truro

Wendell see Orange

Wenham, Town Officers, 1775-1783.

Town of Westfield, Doings of Town Meetings.

WPA Historical Records Survey
Inventories of City and Town Archives

From 1936 to 1943 the Works Projects Administration undertook the Historical Records Survey in all the states. In New England this included inventories of city and town archives. These inventories were not completed in any of the six New England states and only a portion of what was completed was then published. The following is a list of those inventories that were published:

CONNECTICUT
Avon
Berlin
Bloomfield
North Branford
North Haven
Orange
Oxford
Prospect
Seymour
Southbury
Weston

MAINE
Avon
Bar Harbor
Berlin
Brownville
Chesterville
Coplin
Cranberry Isles
Dallas
Eustis
Kennebunkport
Mt. Desert
Seaville
Southwest Harbor
Tremont

MASSACHUSETTS
Agawam
Ashfield
Athol
Auburn
Avon
Ayer
Barre
Bellingham
Berlin
Bernardston
Brookline
Buckland
Chicopee
Clinton
Hampden
Holbrook
Maynard
Warwick

NEW HAMPSHIRE
Atkinson
Auburn
Bedford
Candia
Canterbury
Chester
Exeter
Greenland
New Hampton
Sanbornton

RHODE ISLAND
North Providence
West Greenwich

VERMONT
Albany
Benson
Bolton
Bridgport
Brookline
Cambridge
Castleton
Cavendish
Charlotte
Clarendon
Coventry
Danby
Derby
Eden
Elmore
Essex
Fairfax
Grafton
Grand Isle County
Hubbardton
Hyde Park
Jamaica
Johnson
Mansfield
Morristown
Plymouth
Shrewsbury
Stowe
Tinmouth
Wallingford
Waterville
Wolcott

The POWER and DUTY of TOWNS.

INHABITANTS.

PERSONS of the following description, shall be deemed and taken to be inhabitants of a town or district   (N. N. 12.)   viz.

1. Citizens of the Commonwealth, who before the 10th of April 1767, resided or dwelt within the town for the space of one year, not having been warned to depart therefrom according to law.

2. Such as since the said 10th of April have obtained the approbation of the town or district at a general meeting of the inhabitants for their dwelling there.

3. Such as have obtained a legal settlement by birth, marriage or otherwise, and have not afterwards gained a settlement elsewhere in this or some other of the United States.

4. Every person being a citizen of the Commonwealth who shall be seized of an estate of freehold in the town or district, of the clear annual income of three pounds, and shall reside thereon or within the same town or district, occupying and improving the same in person, for the space of two whole years.

5. Every person, a citizen as aforesaid, who after the age of twenty one years shall reside and pay a town tax for the term of five years successively.

6. Every person a citizen as aforesaid, who shall reside in the town or district, for the space of four years from the ninth of March A. D. 1791, without being legally warned to depart the same.

(See a Law passed, March 6, 1792.)

7. Every such citizen residing and dwelling in any town or district, who shall have and obtain a vote of the same at a regular meeting, to be admitted and received as an inhabitant thereof.

NOTE

TOWNS.   149

NOTE 1. Every woman by intermarrying with an inhabitant, shall be deemed and taken to be an inhabitant of the same town or district with her husband.

2. Children born in wedlock, at their birth and afterwards shall be deemed and taken as inhabitants of the same town or district with their parents.

3. Children otherwise born shall be deemed and taken as inhabitants with the mother until they shall have obtained a legal settlement or habitancy in some other town or district.

4. No person shall have more than one place of legal settlement at one and the same time, but upon obtaining a new place of settlement, shall be deemed and taken to have relinquished any former one.

5. If any inhabitant receive or entertain any person not being an inhabitant, either as an inmate, boarder or tenant, or by any other qualification, for more than ninety days, and do not in writing give information thereof to one or more of the selectmen or the town clerk, of the name of the person thus entertained, with the time he first received him, the place from whence he came, together with such other circumstances respecting such person as have come to his knowledge, he forfeits £5.   N. 468.

6. If any person bring into the Commonwealth any pauper or indigent person, and leave him or her in any town in which he or she is not an inhabitant, he forfeits for every person so brought in and left, the sum of twenty pounds to the use of such town.   N. 469.

7. If masters of vessels arriving with passengers from foreign countries, do not before entry, make return to the office where they shall enter, of the names of such passengers, their nation, age, character and condition, they forfeit at their entry of such vessel and the cargo therein—and are further liable to the forfeiture of fifty pounds. (N. 469.) And if they bring into the Commonwealth any person who has been convicted of any crime, or who is notoriously of a dissolute, infamous and abandoned character, knowing him or her to be such, the vessel in which such person is brought, together with the cargo therein, shall be

N 2   forfeited

Appendix B

The Powers and Duties of Town Officers

The following is abstracted from Samuel Freeman, Esq., *The Town Officer; or the Power and Duty of Selectmen, Town Clerks, Town Treasurers, Overseers of the Poor, Assessors, Constables, Collectors of Taxes, Surveyors of High Ways, Surveyors of Lumber, Fence Viewers, and other Town Officers as Contained in the Laws of the Commonwealth of Massachusetts*, Boston 1793, printed in Boston by I. Thomas and E. T. Andrews, Proprietors of the Work, Faust's Statue, No. 45 Newbury Street.

The Power and Duty of a Moderator (p. 7).

Although this is but an occasional officer, his office is honorable and important. Upon the due execution of it, depends in a great measure, the good order and decorum which ought to be observed in all town meetings . . .

1. Generally to manage and regulate the business of the meeting.

2. When a vote declared by the moderator shall be scrupled, or questioned by seven or more of the voters present, he shall make the vote certain by polling the voters . . .

3. No person shall speak in the meeting, without leave from the moderator . . . and all persons shall be silent at the desire of the moderator, on penalty of five shillings, to the use of the town.

4. If any person shall, after notice from the moderator, persist in his disorderly behavior, the moderator may direct him to withdraw . . . and upon his refusal . . . he shall forfeit twenty shillings or the moderator may order some constable to carry him out of the meeting, and put him into the stocks . . . for the space of three hours, unless the meeting shall sooner adjourn or dissolve.

The Power and Duty of Selectmen (p. 8).

1. To prevent an interference of jurisdiction, the lines between towns shall be run and the marks renewed, once every five years . . . by two or more of the selectmen of each town . . . The selectmen of the most ancient town, to give

notice in writing unto the selectmen of the town adjoining, of the time and place of meeting for such perambulation . . .

2. They shall be overseers of the poor, where other persons shall not be particularly chosen to that office.

3. They or the town clerk, are to make out a list of town officers chosen at the annual March or April meeting, of whom an oath is by law required, and deliver the same to some constable, together with a warrant requiring him to notify them to appear before the town clerk, within seven days from the time of such notice, to take the oaths by law prescribed.

4. They may issue a warrant to a constable for calling town meetings, and they shall insert therein any matter which ten or more freeholders shall desire to have inserted; or they may call a meeting for the express purpose of considering thereof . . .

5. In case of the death, removal or resignation of selectmen, a major part of the survivors, or such as remain in office, may call town meetings.

6. They shall cause the inhabitants of their respective towns, qualified according to the constitution, to be annually warned to meet at such time and place as they shall appoint (being ten days at least before the last Wednesday of May) for the purpose of choosing one or more Representatives . . .

7. They shall call town meetings for the choice of Governor, Lieutenant Governor, Senators and Counsellors, at which meetings they shall impartially preside . . .

8. They may, in the month of January annually, appoint a number of suitable persons for engine men, not exceeding eighteen to any one engine . . .

9. On complaint of any person who should consider himself aggrieved by a water course, they shall view the same, and if they think it reasonable, direct the surveyor to alter the same as they shall think just and proper.

They, or the assessors, shall assign and appoint in writing, annually, to the surveyors of highways, their several limits and divisions of ways, for repair and amendment.

They may consent that surveyors shall employ persons to repair ways, when the sum assessed shall be insufficient, and order fines for default of attending and working, to be expended on such ways.

10. They may by themselves, personally, or by such other person or persons, as they shall appoint, lay out particular or private ways for the use of the town, or of one or more individuals thereof . . . and may agree upon a recompense to any person injured thereby; such ways however not to be established, until reported to, and approved and allowed by the town . . .

11. They are to consider the list of licensed persons transmitted to them by the clerk of the peace, and . . . recommend such as they approve of to be originally licensed, and certify to the court of General Sessions what number of innholders and retailers in their respective towns, they judge to be necessary for the publick good.

They are also to post up in the houses and shops of all taverners, innholders and retailers within the town, a list of the names of all persons reputed common drunkards, tipplers, gamesters, and such as mispend their time and estates in such houses, and if any keeper of such house or shop shall after such notice, suffer any of the persons in such list, to drink or tipple or game therein, or in any of the dependencies thereof, or shall sell them spirituous liquors, he shall forfeit *thirty shillings*. They may forbid all licensed persons in their respective towns to sell spirituous liquors to any person who by idleness or excessive drinking may injure his health, expose himself or family to want or indigent circumstances, or the town to an expense for their maintenance and shall complain of such persons to the judge of probate, in order that guardians may be appointed for them . . .

12. They shall take due care that tythingmen be annually chosen.

13. Being thereto required by the Judge of Probate, they shall make inquisition respecting idiots, lunaticks, or distracted persons.

14. They shall provide from time to time, two boxes for the names of petit jurors, which they shall lock and deliver to the town clerk, and shall once at least in every three years lay before their town a list of such persons as are of good moral character . . . When the inhabitants of a town shall be assembled for the appointment of jurors, the town clerk . . . shall carry the box into the

meeting . . . and shall draw out so many tickets as there are jurymen required by the venire . . .

15. They shall call town meetings for the choice of assessors in the room of such as being duly chosen, refuse to serve, or of constables or collectors who are about to remove out of the commonwealth, and may demand their bills if they refuse to deliver them.

16. They shall be assessors, if none shall be chosen by the town . . .

17. They may file a declaration in the supreme judicial court against absconding constables or collectors.

18. With the assent of two or more Justices of the Peace, they may assign places for the exercising of any of the employments of killing creatures for meat, distilling of spirits, frying of tallow or oil, currying of leather, and making earthen ware, and forbid and restrain the exercise of either of them in other places not so approved . . .

19. In towns where onions shall be shipped they shall appoint some suitable person or persons to weigh the same . . .

20. In every Town where there may be occasion, they shall annually appoint a fit person or persons to be searchers and packers of barreled beef, pork and fish.

21. They, or any of them, shall give a receipt to any person, who may kill a wolf, or wolf's whelp, and bring the head thereof to a constable, who shall in their presence cut off both the ears of the same, and cause them to be burned.

22. When a person shall be committed to the house of correction, the selectmen of the town to which he or she belongs . . . shall at the town's expense, provide suitable materials, and such shall be convenient and necessary to keep the person thus committed, to work during his or her continuance there . . .

23. They shall warn to depart the limits of their town, such persons as shall come to reside therein not entitled to habitancy according to law.

24. It is the duty of the selectmen . . . to use their influence and best endeavours that the youth of their respective towns do regularly attend the schools provided for their instruction, visit and inspect the same, and inquire

into the regulation and discipline thereof . . . and when they are authorised to hire a school master, they shall specially attend to his morals.

25. They are empowered by writing under their hands to approbate auctioneers, for which certificate and record thereof, they are entitled to a fee of six shillings . . .

26. The selectmen of each town where nails are made for sale, shall sometime in the months of March or April annually appoint some suitable person or persons to be inspector or inspectors of nails within such town.

27. They shall annually nominate and appoint a suitable person to be a viewer and sealer of moulds for the making of bricks . . .

28. They may distribute fines incurred by those who refuse to obey the orders of firewards, or neglect their duty when a fire breaks out in any town.

29. They may consent to the digging or breaking up the ground, in any high way, street or lane for the laying, repairing or amending of any drain or common shore.

30. They shall once every month, and oftener, if they see cause, set, ascertain and appoint the assize and weight of all sorts of bread, baked for, or exposed for sale by any baker . . . having respect to the price of grain, meal or flour . . . and making reasonable allowance to bakers, for their charges, pains, and livelihood, which regulations they shall make known in some open and public place or places in the town . . .

31. No building shall be occupied for the business of a sail-maker or rigger, save in such parts of the town as the selectmen shall determine convenient.

32. By a law passed A.D. 1713, no ballast shall be unladen from any ship or other vessel and thrown into any harbour, or taken from any land being the property of any town, without license from the selectmen.

33. When a military watch shall not be ordered and appointed, the justices, together with the selectmen, may order one to be set up, and kept nightly in any town.

34. In every town where tar, pitch, turpentine and resin, are made or vended, they shall choose and appoint a fit person or persons, sometime in the month

of March annually, to be gaugers, viewers and surveyors of the casks made for such commodities . . .

35. They shall annually nominate and appoint meet persons to be wood corders. They shall also annually . . . nominate and appoint meet persons to be measurers and sealers of wood.

36. On application of five or more of the inhabitants, they shall nominate and appoint one or more meet persons to be measurers of wood and bark brought into any town for sale . . .

37. In towns where charcoal is usually sold, they may appoint, as occation shall require, a meet person for seizing and securing baskets for measuring coal . . .

38. They are to have the custody of weights and measures, provided by the constables, and with them are to choose an able man for sealer of such weights and measures . . .

39. To prevent the spreading of the small pox, or other contagious sickness, the selectmen are to take care and make effectual provision for the preservation of the inhabitants, by removing such persons as may be infected therewith to a separate house . . . and by providing nurses, attendance and necessaries at their charge, if able, otherwise at the expense of the town or place to which they belong.

Justices of the peace, with their advice and direction, may impress houses, nurses, attendance and other necessaries for the safety and relief of such sick person, and prevent persons from coming on shore from any vessel visited with such sickness . . .

Persons coming into a town from any place in either of the neighbouring colonies, where the small pox or other malignant infectious distemper is prevailing, shall give notice thereof to the selectmen . . .

The selectmen of any town bordering on either of the neighbouring governments may appoint persons to attend at ferries or other place by which passengers or travellers coming from infected places may pass who may examine such as they shall suspect to bring infection with them, and hinder them from travelling till licensed . . .

When a person in any town is visited with the small pox, the head of the family in which such person is sick, shall acquaint the selectmen therewith, and also hang out on a pole at least six feet in length, a red cloth not under one yard long, and half a yard wide, from the most publick part of the infected house . . .

If any baggage, clothing or other goods be brought to any town, and the selectmen shall have just cause to suspect that the same is infected with the small pox or other infectious distemper, such goods may be secured . . . where there shall be the least danger of the infection spreading . . . there to remain until they shall be sufficiently aired, and be free from infection.

The selectmen may . . . appoint suitable persons to guard a house wherein any person shall be visited with the small pox, who may refrain all persons from going to, or coming from the same without their license . . .

40. They shall at the expense of the town furnish with arms the equipments, such of the inhabitants belonging to the militia as they shall judge to be unable to arm and equip themselves . . .

They may exempt from the train band, by a writing under their hands, such physicians, surgeons, stated school masters, ferrymen and millers, as they shall judge expedient.

When any part of the militia shall be ordered to march for the defence of any state, they shall cause carriages to attend them, with necessary provisions and camp utensils. Penalty for neglect, fifty pounds.

41. Where no justice of the peace dwells, the selectmen may grant license for the tolling of a bell for a funeral on the Lord's day; such license however not to be granted except in cases of necessity.

The Power and Duty of a Town Clerk (p. 34)

1. At the meeting of the inhabitants, upon the first Monday in April, for the purpose of giving in their votes for governor and lieutenant governor, he shall in presence and with the assistance of the selectmen, in open town meeting, sort and count the votes, and form a list of the persons voted for . . .

He shall also make a fair record in presence of the selectmen and in open town meeting, of the name of every person voted for as senators and counsellors . . .

2. He shall truly record all votes passed at any town meeting, during the year for which he is appointed . . .

3. He shall with the moderator of the meeting count and sort the votes given in for a county treasurer . . .

He shall in like manner record and transmit the votes for county register.

4. He, or two of the Selectmen, shall forthwith make out a list of the names of all persons that shall at the annual March or April meeting, be chosen into office, of whom an oath is by law required, and deliver the same to some constable of the town . . . to notify each of the said persons . . .

5. He may administer such oath, and shall make a record of such persons as shall from time to time be sworn into office . . .

6. He shall take care of the jury boxes . . .

7. He is to post up, and enter intentions of marriages, and grant certificates thereof, saving that when the banns of matrimony are forbidden . . . He shall record all marriages certified to him by ministers and justices of the peace, and return a list or copy thereof, to the clerk of the court of the general sessions of the peace . . .

8. He shall at every annual March or April meeting, read the following laws, viz.

> *1. The laws respecting weights and measures.*
> *2. The act to prevent routs, riots, and tumultuous assemblies.*

9. He may certify to the judge of probate, the choice of a guardian made by any minor, living more than ten miles from the judge's dwelling house, if no justice dwell in the town.

10. He may grant summons for witnesses in civil causes.

11. He shall make an entry in a book to be kept for that purpose, of money or goods found, or stray beasts taken up, when notice thereof shall be given to him in writing . . .

He shall once every two months transmit a copy of such entries to the register of deeds and pay to him six pence for each copy.

12. He may issue a precept for selling swine impounded, to recover the forfeiture by law incurred by any persons who shall suffer them to go at large.

13. He may appoint persons to ascertain damages done by creatures impounded, and grant warrants to appraise them, if their owners do not pay such damages.

14. He shall take an account of all persons in his town, that shall be born or die, and register their names in a book, and give a certificate thereof to any who shall desire the same.

15. He shall keep a toll book, and enter therein the marks of all horses that are to be exported, with the names of the persons who last bought them, as well as of the present owner or shipper.

16. He shall enter in his book the certificates of assay masters, respecting the pewter heads and worms, which they may have tried and approved.

17. He may administer an oath to any person who should suspect a dog to be dangerous or mischievous.

The Power and Duty of a Town Treasurer (p. 45)

1. He may apply to the Justices of the Court of General Sessions of the Peace, to summon before them any persons who being chosen to the office of constable, shall refuse to serve, or neglect for the space of seven days to take the oath of office by law prescribed.

2. He may, by complaint to the same court, recover fines incurred by assessor who shall refuse to be sworn.

3. He may sue for the damage done to any public buildings or enclosures, belonging to the town.

4. He shall allow out of the town treasury, the sum of four pounds for every head of a grown wolf, and twenty shillings for every wolf's whelp that may be killed by any person . . .

5. He may recover of any person finding stray money or goods, whereof no owner shall appear in one year and a day, one half the value of the same for the use of the poor.

6. The proceeds of swine sold, are to be placed in the town treasury, there to remain for the owner (deducting one shilling on the pound for the treasurer's trouble) for the space of one year and a day, and if not then claimed, to be disposed of, one half to the impounder, and the other half to the poor of the town, to be distributed by the treasurer.

7. He is to receive all sums duly assessed upon the inhabitants of his town, for their use, and pay out the same agreeable to the legal orders of the town.

8. He may issue a warrant of distress . . . against any constable or collector who shall neglect to collect and pay the sums committed to him to collect.

And against a sheriff or deputy Sheriff who should neglect to make due return of such warrants.

9. By the law which made the first provision for the choice of a town treasurer, passed A.D. 1699, he is empowered to demand and receive all debts, rents and dues belonging to the town or the poor thereof . . . and to pay out such monies according to order from the selectmen, or overseers of the poor. . . . And every treasurer shall annually make and render to the town a true account of all his receipts and payments: And shall have such allowance for his service, as shall be agreed and ordered by the town.

The Power and Duty of Overseers of the Poor (p. 49)

1. They are to take care of and comfortably provide for the support and maintenance of persons who are unable to support themselves, at the charge and expense of the town whereof they are inhabitants, or at that of the commonwealth, if they be not inhabitants of any town within the same, unless they have one or more relations within the commonwealth, in the line or degree of father or grand father, mother or grand mother, children, or grand children, who are of sufficient ability to support them.

2. They may with the assent of two justices of the peace, set to work, or bind out apprentice, all such children whose parents shall in their opinion be

unable to maintain them, whether they receive alms or are chargeable to the town, or not, in case they be not taxed.

3. They shall make enquiry into the treatment of children, bound out by themselves or their predecessors in office, and if they find them injured, seek redress.

4. They may also with the assent of two justices, set to work or bind out to service, for the space of one whole year at a time, all such persons, married or unmarried, upwards of twenty years of age, able of body, who have no visible means of support, and live idly, and neither use or exercise any lawful trade or ordinary calling for a subsistence, and employ the proceeds of their labour for the support of their families, or in case they have no families, for their own benefit.

5. They may issue an order for the discharge of any person committed to the house of correction, when it shall appear to them, that the ends of such commitment have been answered.

The Power and Duty of Assessors (p. 53)

1. They, or the selectmen, shall assign and appoint in writing annually, to the surveyors of Highways, their several limits and divisions of ways for repair and amendment of the same.

2. They shall assess the sums voted by the town for repair and amendment of such ways, and deliver to the surveyors, a list of the persons within their respective limits, and the sums in which they are assessed.

3. They shall assess in a distinct column in the next assessment for a town tax, the sums contained in any lists rendered to them by the surveyor, of persons who may have been deficient in working out or paying the highway rate.

4. They shall assess, in manner by law directed, all such rates and taxes as the general court shall order and appoint their town to pay towards the charges of the government . . .

5. They shall make a perfect list or lists of their assessments, under their hands, or the hands of the major part of them, and commit the same to the

constables or collectors, if any there be, otherwise to the sheriff or his deputy, with a warrant as by law prescribed to collect the same.

6. They shall return a certificate of their assessments to the treasurer of the commonwealth . . .

7. Before they commit their assessments to the constables, &c. as aforesaid, they shall have the same recorded in the town or district book, or leave an exact copy thereof by them signed, with the town or district clerk . . . and at the same time shall lodge in the said clerk's office the invoice or valuation, or a copy thereof, from whence the rates or assessments are made, that the inhabitants may inspect the same.

8. If they shall not observe the legal warrants of the treasurer or receiver general by them received, for assessing any rate or tax, they shall forfeit and pay the full sum in such warrant mentioned; which shall be levied by distress and sale of their effects.

9. They shall assess all county, town, and parish taxes, according to the rules that shall be prescribed in the last tax out of the general court . . .

10. Before they make any assessment, they shall give seasonable warning to the inhabitants at any of their respective meetings, or by posting up notifications in some public place . . .

11. They shall make reasonable abatements to any persons who shall make it appear to them that they are overrated: If they refuse so to do, such aggrieved persons may apply for relief to the next court of general sessions of the peace . . .

12. They may apportion on the polls and estates such additional sum over and above the precise sum to them committed to assess, as any fractional divisions thereof may render convenient in the apportionment, not exceeding five per cent on the sum taxed . . .

13. They may add to any of their other taxes, their town's proportion of a county tax, when it would be inconvenient to make a separate list.

14. When a constable or collector shall be remiss in his duty in not levying and paying to the treasurer or receiver general . . . and shall not have any estate whereon to make distress . . . the assessors (having notice thereof in

writing from the treasurer) shall without any other or further warrant assess such deficiency upon the inhabitants in the same manner as the sum committed to such deficient collector . . .

15. In case of the decease of any constable or collector, they may appoint some suitable person to compleat his collections.

16. They may file a declaration in the supreme judicial court against any absconding constable or collector.

17. They may procure and appoint in writing under their hands, some suitable person a collector to prefect the collections of a constable or collector who may become *non compos mentis* who hath a guardian duly appointed, or of one who by bodily infirmities is rendered incapable of discharging the duties of his office. If he request them so to do . . .

The Power and Duty of Constables (p. 67)

1. They are to warn town meetings, having a warrant from the selectmen, or the major part of them, for that purpose.

2. A constable having received a warrant from the town clerk, or two of the selectmen, shall, within three days from the time of receiving the same, summon the town officers chosen at the annual March or April meeting, of whom an oath is by law required, to appear before the town clerk within seven days, and take the oath . . . for which service, as well as for other town business, the town shall make him a reasonable allowance.

3. Persons chosen Representatives, are to be notified, of their choice, by a constable of the town.

4. A constable, upon receiving a warrant from the clerk of the Supreme Court, or Court of General Sessions of the Peace, shall notify town meetings for the appointment of grand jurors . . .

5. He is also in like manner to notify the freeholders and other inhabitants qualified to vote for Representatives, and particularly the selectmen and town clerk, to assemble and be present at the appointment of petit jurors . . .

6. Constables are to inform some Justice of the Peace of any person, who shall profanely curse or swear, in their hearing, if he be known to them: if not they

shall apprehend him, and forthwith carry him before some Justice of the Peace; on penalty of 40s.

7. They shall take due notice, and prosecute all breaches of the act for the due observation of the Lord's day.

8. If any persons to the number of twelve or more, being armed with clubs or other weapons; or if any number of persons, consisting of thirty or more, shall be unlawfully, routously, riotously, or tumultuously assembled, it is the duty of a constable, among the rioters, or as near them as he can safely come, to command silence, and make proclamation in these or the like words:

Commonwealth of Massachusetts

By virtue of an act of this Commonwealth . . . I am directed to charge and command . . . all persons being here assembled, immediately to disperse themselves, and peaceably to depart to their habitations, or to their lawful business, upon the pains inflicted by said act.

God save the Commonwealth

9. A constable to whom the head of a wolf or wolf's whelp, killed by any person, shall be brought, shall in the presence of one or more of the selectmen, cut off both the ears of the same, and cause them to be burned.

10. A constable to whom the warrant of a Coroner for summoning a jury of inquest shall be directed, shall forthwith execute the same, and repair to the place where the dead body shall be . . .

11. A constable may serve, in any town to which he belongs, any writ or execution in any personal action where the damage sued for or recovered, shall not exceed twenty pounds.

12. Constables are also by law empowered, and required, to serve warrants issuing from a Justice of the Peace, and also warrants from the selectmen, to warn persons out of town.

13. If no collector be chosen in any town . . . the constable or constables shall gather the rates and taxes . . .

14. When in the execution of their office, for the preservation of the peace, or for the apprehending or securing any person or persons for violating the

same, or for any other criminal matter or cause, they may require suitable aid and assistance therein; and if any person being thereto required shall refuse such aid, he shall forfeit a sum not exceeding 40s.

15. Having orders in writing from the Justices of the Peace, and selectmen of the town . . . they are to warn a watch or watches to be kept nightly, see that all persons so warned, attend and observe their duty in that regard, give in charge to the watch to see that all disorders of the night be prevented and suppressed, examine all persons walking abroad in the night after ten o'clock, and secure suspicious persons until the morning, and then carry them before a Justice of the Peace.

16. It is the duty of constables, to use their utmost endeavours, to prevent the drawing of any unlawful lottery.

17. By a law passed A.D. 1725, they have power and authority, in the execution of the warrants or writs to them directed by lawful authority, to convey as well any prisoner or prisoners . . . either to the Justice issuing such warrant or writ, or to the common goal of the county . . .

18. Constables are to see that their respective towns be provided with the following weights and measures, viz.

> *One bushel; one half bushel; one peck; one half peck; one ale quart; one wine pint and half pint; one ell; one yard; one set of brass weights to four pounds . . .*

Constables of sea port towns are also to provide, at the town's charge, one hundred weight; one half hundred; one quarter of an hundred; and one fourteen pounds weight . . .

Persons exempted from serving in the office of a constable are

1. Such as have served as constable, or collector, within seven years.
2. Persons in commission for any office, civil or military.
3. Church officers.
4. Members of the Council, Senate, or House of Representatives.

Appendix B

The Power and Duty of Collectors of Taxes (p. 76)

1. They shall collect all such rates or taxes as by a warrant from the selectmen or assessors shall be committed to them to collect; and pay in the same according to the directions in such warrant.

2. If any person refuse to pay the sum in which he is assessed, the collector has power to distrain his goods or chattels, and after the space of four days to sell the same at public auction, giving public notice of such sale, forty eight hours previous thereto . . . or if such persons do not within twelve days after demand thereof, shew the collector sufficient goods whereby the said assessment may be levied, he may take his body and commit him to the common goal . . .

3. Collectors may also demand, distrain and apprehend, in any other town or place to which any person assessed may remove . . . and in case of such removal, they may, after three months notice, sell so much of the real estate . . . as will amount to the sum he is assessed . . .

4. They may also sell at public auction, and thereof give deeds to the purchasers . . . so much of the unimproved lands of non resident proprietors, or improved lands of proprietors living out of the limits of the Common-wealth, as will be sufficient to discharge the taxes laid upon them . . .

5. When taxes are made payable at two or more times or days of payment, and the persons assessed shall be about to remove, collectors may demand and levy the whole sum . . .

6. Their power continues until they have perfected their collections, although new ones may be chosen and sworn.

7. If they be hindered, or impeded in collecting the taxes committed to them, they have power to require aid, and persons who being thereto required shall refuse their aid, shall forfeit a sum not exceeding 40s.

8. Having a warrant from a Justice of the Peace, they may distrain the goods of an owner of improved lands, who shall not reside or be an inhabitant of the town where such lands lie . . .

9. In case of commitment, the collector shall give to the keeper of the prison an attested copy of his warrants, and thereupon certify under his hand the

sum due from the person committed, and that he has taken his body for want of goods whereon to make distress.

10. When any person is taxed for real estate in his possession, whereof he is not the owner, the collector shall demand of him the amount of such taxes . . .

11. Their fees, in cases of distress or commitment, are the same which sheriffs by law are entitled to for levying executions, viz. for the first £20, or under, eight pence a pound, above and not exceeding £40, four pence, a pound, above that, and not exceeding £100, two pence a pound, and for all above £100, one penny a pound.

12. When a collector, who is about to remove out of the Commonwealth, shall refuse to deliver his bills and monies by him collected . . . he shall pay a fine of sixty pounds . . .

13. If collectors be negligent and remiss in their duty of levying and paying the sums committed to them, the treasurer . . . may issue warrants of distress against them . . .

14. In case of the decease of any collector, his executors or administrators shall within two months, settle with the assessors . . . in default thereof shall be chargeable with the whole sum committed to such collector . . .

15. Collectors committed to goal for default in payment of taxes shall be admitted to the liberty of the yard.

16. Distress shall not in any case be made or taken from any person, of arms or household utensils, necessary for upholding life, nor of tools nor implements, necessary for his trade or occupation, beasts of the plough, necessary for the cultivation of his improved lands, nor of bedding nor apparell, necessary for himself or his family.

17. When collectors are taken on execution, they shall deliver to the assessors on demand, a copy of all the assessments in their hands unsettled, with the evidence of all pacents made thereon . . .

18. If a collector abscond or secrete himself for the space of a month, the selectmen may file a declaration against him at the Supreme Judicial Court.

19. Collectors shall once every two months at least exhibit to the selectmen a just and true account of all the monies they have received . . .

20. When any person shall abscond, they may have like remedy against his agent, factor or trustee, for recovery of his rates, as other creditors have for recovery of their debts.

21. When any person rated, shall die, or remove out of town, or where any unmarried woman who is rated shall intermarry, collectors may sue for such rates . . .

22. Their warrant against poor persons who may have been committed to goal and discharged upon taking the oath by law prescribed, shall remain good, and may be carried into execution against the goods or estate which may then or afterwards belong to such poor person . . .

23. They shall be holden to pay the tax of any person imprisoned and discharged, as in the last article, unless such imprisonment be made within a year, or, unless the town abate the same.

Persons exempted from serving as a Collector are

> 1. Any one who has served as constable or collector, for himself or his own turn, within the space of seven years.
> 2. Persons in commission for any office civil or military.
> 3. Church officers.
> 4. Members of the Council, Senate, or House of Representatives.
> 5. Selectmen, town clerk, town treasurer or assessors for the time being.

The Power and Duty of Surveyors of the Highways (p. 84)

1. They have the power and authority to cut down, lop off, dig up and remove, all sorts of trees, bushes, stones, fences, rails, gates, bars, inclosures, or other matter or thing, that shall in any way straiten, hurt, hinder or incommode the highway, or townway, and also to dig for stone, gravel, clay, marle, sand, or earth, in any land not planted or inclosed, and the materials thus dug up to remove to such place or places in the highways, for the repair and amendment thereof, as they shall determine necessary.

2. No surveyor of highways shall cause any water course, occasioned by the wash of any highway or townway, to be so conveyed by the side of such

highway as to incommode any person, house, store, shop, or other building, or to obstruct any person in the prosecution of his business . . .

3. A surveyor shall give reasonable notice, in writing if desired, to each person in his list, of the sum he is assessed to the highways or townways, and also to the inhabitants within his district . . . six days notice . . . of the times and places he shall appoint, for providing materials, and labouring; to the end, that each person may have opportunity to work on the highways and townways, in person, or by his substitute, or with his oxen, horses, cart and plough, at the rates and prices the town shall affix to such labour . . . or he may pay the surveyor in money the sum he is assessed . . .

4. He shall at the expiration of his term, render to the assessors a list of such persons as shall have been deficient, in working out or otherwise paying their highway rate.

5. When the sum assessed for the repair of highways and townways, shall be insufficient for the purpose, the surveyors, with the consent of the selectmen, shall employ persons to make up the deficiency, who shall be paid therefore out of the town treasury.

6. If any town shall neglect to vote or agree upon a sum to be assessed for the express purpose of repairing and amending such ways, and shall not otherways effectually provide therefor, each surveyor shall assign to the several persons in his limits, their rateable proportion of days work, and of cart, team and plough, as near as he can, and shall assign certain days of the business, and give notice thereof to the persons in his limits, upwards of sixteen years of age, and liable by law to be taxed, six days at least before the time assigned, to attend the service with suitable tools, and with carts and teams . . .

The Power and Duty of Surveyors and Measurers of Boards, Plank, Timber, and Slitwork (p. 90)

1. They shall new mark all such of the said articles, of the measure whereof they shall have any doubt, having due consideration for drying and shrinking; and shall make reasonable allowance for rots, knots, and splits.

2. They may sue those persons who ship off boards before they be surveyed, and may have one half of the forfeiture recovered.

Note I. *The dimensions of boards for exportation are not less than one inch in thickness, and ten feet in length, and they must be square edged . . .*

The Power and Duty of Surveyors of Shingles and Clapboards (p. 91)

1. Before any of these articles shall be shipped, they shall be viewed and surveyed by a sworn surveyor, who shall be allowed by the buyer six pence for every thousand, for surveying and telling.

Shingles
On the hoop of every bundle of shingles the town brand shall be set.

No shingles shall be offered for sale under the following dimensions, viz. All shingles shall be split cross ways the grain, and be eighteen inches long, unless those made for home use; pine shingles shall be free from sap, and all shingles shall be free from shakes and worm holes, and shall be half an inch thick at the butt end, when green, and full three eighths of an inch when thoroughly seasoned, if for exportation to a foreign market . . . and four inches and half wide on an average, and none less that three inches wide . . . and each bundle shall contain two hundred and fifty shingles . . .

Clapboards
All pine clapboards that shall be exposed to sale shall be made of good sound timber, clear of sap, and all clapboards shall be free from shakes and worm holes, and of the following dimensions, viz. full five eighths of an inch on the back or thickest part, five inches wide, and four feet six inches long, and they shall be strait and well shaved . . .

The Power and Duty of Viewers and Cullers of Staves and Hoops (p. 92)

1. All staves that shall be exported beyond sea, shall be first culled, and all hoops viewed and surveyed: and a certificate shall be given by the culler or surveyor, of the quantity by him culled and surveyed; and the bands with

which the bundles of the hoops are bound, shall be sealed with the town brand.

2. Viewers and cullers of staves and hoops may sue for the penalties incurred by those who shall ship either of those articles, before they are culled or surveyed, and shall be entitled to half the forfeiture recovered.

Staves
No staves or hoops shall be offered for sale, that shall be under the following dimensions, viz. All white oak butt staves, shall be at least five feet in length, five inches wide, and one inch and a quarter thick on the heart, or thinest edge, and every part thereof. And all white oak pine staves shall be at least four feet and eight inches in length, four inches broad in the narrowest part, and not less than three quarters of an inch thick on the heart, or thinest edge.
. . .

Hoops
All hogshead hoops that shall be exposed to sale, or exported, shall be from ten to thirteen feet in length, and shall be made of white oak or walnut, and of good and sufficient substance, well shaved; those made of oak, shall be not less than one inch broad at the least end, and those made of walnut shall be not less than three quarters of an inch broad at the least end; each bundle shall consist of thirty hoops . . .

For their time and service they shall be allowed as follows, viz. One shilling and eight pence per thousand for barrel staves, two shillings per thousand for hogshead staves, two shillings and four pence per thousand for pipe staves, and two shillings and eight pence per thousand for but staves . . . three shillings per thousand for hoops . . .

The Power and Duty of Fence Viewers (p. 94)

1. If an occupant of land, neglect or refuse to repair or rebuild the fence which of right he ought to maintain, the aggrieved party may apply to two or more fence viewers to survey the same, and upon their determination that the fence is insufficient, they shall signify the same in writing to the occupant, and direct him to repair or rebuild the same within six days, and in default thereof, the complainant may make up the same, and may demand of him

double the sum at which the fence viewers may in writing, value the fence so made, together with their fees.

Note. *All fences of four feet high, and in good repair, consisting of rails, timber, boards or stone walls; and also brooks, rivers, ponds, creeks, ditches and hedges, or other matter or thing equivalent thereto in the judgement of the fence viewer, shall be accounted legal and sufficient fences.*

2. On application of any person with whom a dispute shall arise about the respective occupant right in partition fences, and his or their obligation to maintain the same. They may, after due notice, assign to each party, his share thereof in writing; which assignment being recorded in the town clerk's office . . .

3. When lands occupied by different persons are bounded by a brook, pond or creek, which of itself is not a sufficient fence, and it is impracticable without great expense to make the fence in the middle or true boundary line, two or more fence viewers on application to them made, shall forthwith view such brook, river, pond or creek, and having given previous notice to the parties, may in writing determine where the fence shall be set up and maintained.

4. Where lands belonging to two persons in severalty shall have been improved in common and one of the occupants shall desire to improve his part in severalty and the other occupant shall refuse to divide the line where the fence ought to be built, or to build a sufficient fence on his part of the line when divided. They may, on complaint of the occupant, divide the same . . .

The Power and Duty of Tythingmen (p. 102)

1. Tythingmen have power, and it is their duty carefully to inspect all licensed houses, and to inform of all disorders or misdemeanors which they shall discover or know to be committed in them, to a justice of the Peace, or to the General Sessions of the county; and also of all such as shall sell spirituous liquors without license.

2. They shall also inform of all idle and disorderly persons, profane swearers and the like offenders, to the end they may be punished.

3. They may enter into any of the rooms or other parts of an inn or public house of entertainment, on the Lord's Day, and the evening preceding and succeeding. (*If any landlord or licensed person refuse such entrance he forfeits 40s.*)

4. They may examine all persons whom they shall have good cause, from the circumstances thereof, to suspect of unnecessary travelling on said day - and to demand of all such persons the cause thereof, together with their names and place of abode . . .

5. They are held and obliged by law to enquire into, and inform of all offences against the act providing for the due observation of the Lord's Day, passed March 8, 1792. The substance of which act is as follows, viz.

> 1. That no person shall keep open his shop, warehouse or workhouse, nor shall upon land or water do any manner of labour, business, or work (works of necessity and charity only excepted) nor be present at any concert of music, dancing, or any public diversion, shew, or entertainment, nor use any sport, game, play, or recreation . . .
> 2. That no traveller, drover, waggoner, teamster, or any of their servants, shall travel on the Lord's day . . .
> 3. That no vintner, retailer of strong liquors, or innholder, or other person keeping a house of public entertainment, shall entertain or suffer any of the inhabitants of the town . . . not being travellors, strangers, or lodgers in such houses, to abide and remain in their houses, yards, orchards, or fields, drinking or spending their time either idly or at play, or doing any secular business on the Lord's day . . .
> 4. That no person shall be present at any concert of music, dancing or other public diversion, nor shall any person or persons use any game, sport, play, or recreation, on the land or water, on the evening next preceding or succeeding the Lord's day . . .
> 5. That any person being able of body, and not otherwise necessarily prevented, who shall, for the space of three months together, absent him or herself from the public worship of God on the Lord's day, providing there be any place of worship at which he or she can conscientiously and conveniently attend,

shall pay a fine of 10s.

6. That if any person shall on the Lord's day, within the walls of any house of public worship, behave rudely or indecently, he or she shall pay a fine not more than 40s. nor less than 5s.

7. That if any person either on the Lord's day, or at any other time, shall wilfully interrupt, or disturb, any assembly of people met for the public worship of God, within the place of their assembly or out of it, he or they shall severally pay a fine not exceeding £10, nor less than 20s.

8. That no person shall execute any civil process from midnight preceding to midnight following the Lord's day . . .

The Power and Duty of Firewards (p. 105)

1. Firewards shall have for a distinguishing badge of their office, a staff of five feet long, painted red, and headed with a bright brass spire, six inches long.

2. On notice of a fire, they shall immediately repair to the place . . . and vigorously exert themselves in requiring and procuring assistance to extinguish and prevent the spreading of the fire, and for the pulling down, or blowing up of any houses, or any other service relating thereto, as they may be directed by two or three of the chief civil or military officers of the town, to put a stop to the fire, and in removing household stuff, goods and merchandizes out of any dwelling houses, store houses, or other buildings actually on fire, or in danger thereof, in appointing guards to secure and take care of the same, and to suppress all tumults and disorders - and due obedience is required to be yeilded to them, and each of them, for that service, on penalty of 40s . . .

The Power and Duty of Clerks of the Market (p. 106)

1. Clerks of the market . . . may in the day time enter into any house, stall, bake house, out house or ware house, belonging to any baker or seller of bread, there to search for, view, weigh or try all or any the bread of such person, or which shall there be found: And if any bread shall there be found wanting either in the goodness of the stuff whereof the same shall be made, or

in the due working or baking thereof, or shall be deficient in the due weight, or shall not be truly marked according to law, or shall be of any other sort than the law allows, they may seize and take the same, and cause it to be given and distributed to the poor of the town . . .

Note   *1. The assize of bread is to be ascertained by the selectmen.*

2. Every person who bakes or makes bread for sale, shall fairly mark or imprint . . . such distinct mark as shall be appointed or allowed by the selectmen, so that his bread may be known and distinguished . . .

The Power and Duty of Searchers and Sealers of Leather (p. 107)

1. They shall have two several marks or seals, to be prepared by the town, with one of which they shall seal all such leather as they shall find well and sufficiently tanned, and with the other all such leather, as they shall find well and sufficiently curried, according to law.

2. Sealers of leather have power ex officie to make search and view in any house, shop, warehouse, or other place where they may conceive any leather to be, whether wrought into shoes, boots, or other wares or not, and seize all leather whether so wrought or not, which they shall find not tanned, curried, or sealed as the law directs; and may retain the same (if the owner submit not to their judgment) until trial thereof be had, and judgment given . . .

Of Tanning Leather

It is provided, by a law passed A.D. 1698, and yet in force, that no person exercising this trade or mystery, shall put to sale any kind of leather which shall be insufficiently tanned, or which has been over limed, or burnt in the limes, or which shall not have been after the tanning thereof, well and thoroughly dried, nor set any of his fats in tan hills or other places where the woozes or leather put to tan in the same, may take any unkind hears, nor shall put any leather into any hot or warm woozes whatsoever, on penalty of £20, for every such offence.

Of Currying Leather

No person exercising this mystery shall curry any kind of leather, except it be sealed, nor any hide not thoroughly dried, after his wet season, in which wet season, he shall not use any stale urine, or any other deceitful or subtle mixture, thing, way, or means to corrupt or hurt the same, nor shall curry any kind of leather meet for outer sole leather, with any other than good hard tallow, nor with any less of that than the leather will receive, nor shall curry any kind of leather meet for upper leather and inward soles, but with good and sufficient stuff, being fresh and not salt, and thoroughly liquored till it will receive no more; nor shall burn or sealled any hide or leather in the currying, but shall work the same sufficiently in all points and respects, on pain of forfeiting, for each offence, every such hide marred, or hurt by his evil workmanship or handling . . .

The Power and Duty of a Sealer of Weights and Measures (p. 109)

1. He is to send out his warrant sometime in the month of *May* annually, directed to the constable or constables, requiring him or them to warn all the inhabitants to bring in to him, to be proved and sealed, all the weights and measures, and great and small beams which they make use of, at such time and place as he shall appoint.

2. He shall deface and destroy all such weights and measures, as cannot be brought to their just standard.

3. He may go to the houses of such of the inhabitants, as, upon warning given agreeably to law, shall neglect to bring or send in their beams, weights and measures to be proved and sealed, at the place assigned for that purpose, and shall there prove and seal the same.

4. It is his duty to go to the houses, or store houses, of merchants and others that usually weigh with great beams and weights, and there prove and seal the same . . .

Their fees are--

>1. One penny for every beam, weight, and measure, which they may find conformable to the town standard, and two pence when they shall find the same not conformable to said standard.
>2. Three pence when they go to the owner's house, or when the beams, weights or measures are brought to be proved or sealed at any

other time than on the day assigned by the sealer.

3. For proving and sealing great beames and weights, at merchants houses or store houses, their reasonable charge for carrying the standards, and eight pence per hour for their time in attending that service . . .

5. He is to seal baskets used and improved in measuring charcoal, brought into town for sale, which basket shall be of the following dimensions, viz. seventeen inches and a half deep . . . and nineteen inches in breadth . . .

The Duty of a Viewer and Sealer of Moulds for the making of Bricks (p. 112)

1. He may from time to time, enter into all brick yards to view their moulds and to see that they be of due size, well shod with iron, and sealed as the law directs, and if he find them under size, or not well shod, he may break the same.

2. Every brick maker, before the fitting of his kiln, shall call the viewer to oversee his bricks, who shall forthwith attend the service, and be paid two pence per thousand for all bricks by him viewed, and one penny for each mould by him sealed.

Note. *Clay for the making of bricks shall be digged before the 10th of December yearly, and shall be turned over in the month of February or March next ensuing, at least twenty days before it be wrought, and then well and thoroughly wrought.*

And no person shall temper his clay with salt or brackish water; nor dig any clay in any place where thesalt water comes in.

Size of Bricks
Nine inches long; four and a quarter broad; two and a half thick . . . .

The Power and Duty of Assay Masters (p. 113)

1. They shall inspect and make trial of all heads and worms used in distilling strong liquors, that shall be suspected by them, and if upon their assaying and trial of them, they be found to be made of lead or other base metal, or to have

an alloy of lead or of other base metal in them, they shall give notice thereof to the distiller or owner thereof, who shall in such case make no further use thereof, under the penalty of £100.

2. They may enter into any still house or place where such utensils are suspected to be kept, and cut off so much of them as shall be needful to make an assay or trail of them . . .

The Power and Duty of Wood Corders (p. 114)

1. All cord wood exposed to sale, shall be four feet long, accounting to half the cars; and the cord being well and close laid together, shall measure eight feet in length, and four feet in height.

2. If any firewood brought into any town by water be less in length, it shall be forfeited, two thirds to the use of the poor, and one third to the sealer of wood (fee under the power and duty of a measurer and sealer of wood).

3. Wood corders may demand and receive three pence per cord for all wood that shall be corded by them . . .

The Power and Duty of Measurers and Sealers of Wood (p. 114)

1. They may seize all wood brought into any town by water that shall be less in length than four feet including half the cars, and the same shall be forfeited, one third to the sealer, and the other two thirds to the poor of the town.

2. No wharfinger, or carter, shall cart or carry from any wharf, or landing place (except for his own use and consumption) any firewood that shall be less in length than four feet aforesaid, nor until it be measured by a measurer and sealer of wood, on penalty of 6s.

3. Wharfingers shall be chargable to measurers of wood, for their fees (if demanded) and compellable by law to pay the same . . .

Appendix B

The Power and Duty of Measurers of Wood and Bark (p. 115)

1. They are to measure loads of wood and bark brought into town for sale, and give the driver thereof a ticket of the same, certifying the quantity of wood such load contains.

2. They shall prosecute for the forfeiture of such wood or bark as may be offered for sale before it be first measured, two thirds whereof is to go to the use of the poor, and the other third to their own use.

3. They shall receive such fees or allowance for their services as the selectmen shall judge reasonable . . .

The Power and Duty of Deer Reeves (p. 119)

It is the duty of deer reeves to inquire into and inform some Justice of the Peace of all offences against the act passed A.D. 1764, for the preservation and increase of moose and deer - the purport of which is as follows, viz.

That every person who shall kill any moose or deer between the 21st of December and the 11th of August in any year, or have the flesh or raw skin of any moose or deer killed within that time, in his possession, and be thereof convicted, he shall for each moose or deer so killed, and for each raw skinn or the flesh of any moose or deer, killed within the time aforesaid, found in his possession, pay a fine of £6, one moiety of which is to be for the use of the government, and the other moiety to the informer . . .

The Power and Duty of Gaugers, Viewers and Surveyors of Casks made for Tar, Pitch, Turpentine and Rosin (p. 120)

1. They are not only to gauge the casks before they be filled, but to search and prove them afterwards, and mark, with such mark as the selectmen shall appoint, such as they shall find merchantable and of due assize.

Note. *The gauge or assize is as follows, viz. Barrels for* tar *to be* thirty two gallons, *and half barrels* sixteen gallons, *and none under. Casks for* pitch, turpentine *and* rosin *to be* thirty five gallons, *and made of sound, well seasoned* timber, and each cooper is to set his brand mark on all his casks made for these commodities.

2. They shall at all seasonable times, on due notice, attend and perform the service of gauging casks, and surveying tar, pitch, turpentine and rosin, by cleansing the tar of water, and filling the cask with good tar; and examining the turpentine by broaching it on the head opposite the bung, for the better discovery of dirt and chips, and over great bungs and other frauds; and also to see that the rosin and pitch be well made, and the cask well filled, and without deceit, after the best manner that may be, and to mark such cask of the said commodities as they shall find merchantable.

Their fees are sixteen pence per ton for the casks they shall gauge, survey and mark, to be paid by the cooper that employs them; two shillings per ton for such casks of tar, pitch, rosin and turpentine as they shall examine and mark, besides three pence per mile for travel, above one mile, and they may detain so much of the commodity as will satisfy the same, and if not redeemed in 24 hours, expose it to sale . . .

The Power and Duty of Surveyors, Gaugers and Searchers of Tar, Pitch, Turpentine, and Rosin (p. 121)

Officers of this description are appointed by the Court of General Sessions of the Peace.

Their duty is (when desired) to view, gauge and search all such casks of the said commodities as shall be presented to their view, and mark each cask they may find merchantable, on the fairest head, with such mark as the Sessions may appoint.

Their fees are *two pence* each cask . . .

The Power and Duty of Measurers of Salt (p. 122)

Measurers of salt are to be appointed yearly by the Justices of the Court of General Sessions of the Peace, and are to measure all salt that shall be imported and sold out of any ship, or other vessel, and shall be entitled to three half pence for every hogshead of salt so measured, to be paid, the one half by the buyer, the other half by the seller. . . .

The Power and Duty of Measurers of Grain (p. 122)

1. They are to be appointed in sea port towns by the Court of General Sessions of the Peace, and at all times shall attend at the request of the buyer of any wheat to measure the same, and shall weigh as many bushels as either the buyer or seller shall desire; and from the mean weight shall determine whether the wheat be of greater or less weight than the legal standard . . .

2. There fees are -- one half penny per bushel for any quantity not exceeding 20 bushels; above that and not exceeding 50 bushels, one half penny per bushel . . . If the quantity exceed 50 bushels, one farthing only per bushel . . .

3. They shall be provided at the expense of the town with two half bushel measures . . . and with proper scales and weights to weigh at least one bushel at a time.

The Power and Duty of Searchers and Packers of Barreled Beef, Pork and Fish (p. 123)

1. They shall pack and search all the fish, beef and pork which shall be packed in the town designed for exportation out of the state, and they shall not pack any in a cask made of unseasoned stuff . . .

2. Where such commodities are packed up for sale, they shall previously thereto see that they be properly repacked, and that there be good salt in each cask, sufficient to preserve the fish, beef and pork from damage . . .

3. It is their business to see that the beef and pork in casks be of the whole, half and quarter, and so proportionally, that the best be not left out . . .

4. On all casks of beef, pork and fish, searched, examined and approved as aforesaid, the packer shall brand or imprint, with a burning iron, the following brand or mark MASS. RPD. with the initial letters of his Christian name, and his Surname at large, and the letter P. at the end thereof . . .

5. All such other provision as he shall find wholesome and useful, though for its quality it be not merchantable, he shall cause to be well packed, salted and filled, and the same mark with the word REFUSE . . .

The Power and Duty of Cullers of Dry Fish (p. 125)

Cullers of dry fish shall, in the exercise of their duty, have regard to the contract between the buyer and the seller, with respect to the season of the year wherein such fish is cured.

They are entitled to receive of the purchaser, one penny half penny for every quintal of fish which they survey, or cull.

The Power and Duty of Engine Men (p. 125)

1. Engine men may meet together sometime in May annually, for the purpose of choosing a master or director of the engine, and establishing such rules and regulations for the well ordering of the company, as the selectmen of the town shall judge necessary and approve.

2. They are to meet together once at least in each month, and oftener if necessary, for the purpose of examining the state of the engine and the appendages belonging to the same, and seeing that the engine be in good repair, and ready to proceed on any emergency to the relief of any part of the community who may be invaded by the calamity of fire.

3. They are obliged to go forward, either by night or by day, and use their best endeavors, to extinguish any fire that may happen in the town . . .

They are excused from all military duty . . .

The Power and Duty of a Weigher of Onions (p. 126)

1. It is the duty of a weigher of onions, to weigh bunches of onions which are to be shipped or exported out of the Commonwealth, and to give certificates of the weight . . .

2. He is intitled to eight pence for every hundred bunches weighed . . . His fees are to be paid by the purchaser . . .

The Power and Duty of Overseers of a Work House (p. 126)

1. Overseers of a work house have the inspection and government thereof, with full power of appointing a master and needful assistants, for the more immediate care and oversight of the persons received into or employed in the same.

2. They are once in every month, and at other times, as occasion shall require, to assemble together for the purpose of determining the most elligible method of discharging the duties of their office.

3. At their stated meetings they have power to make needful orders and regulations for such house, which orders shall be binding until the next public meeting of the inhabitants of the town which provided the same . . .

4. They, or any two of them, shall commit to such house, by writing under their hands, to be employed and governed according to the rules and orders of the house, all poor and indigent persons, that are maintained by, or receive alms from the town; also all persons able of body to work, and not having estate or means otherwise to maintain themselves, who refuse or neglect so to do, live a dissolute, vagrant life, and exercise no ordinary calling or lawful business, sufficient to gain them an honest livelihood, and all such as having some rateable estate, but not sufficient to qualify them to vote in town affairs, do neglect the due care and improvement thereof, and such as spend their time and property in publick houses, to the neglect of their proper business, or by otherwise mispending what they earn, to the impoverishment of themselves and their families, are likely to become chargeable to the town or to the Commonwealth . . .

The Power and Duty of Hogreeves (p. 130)

The general duty of hogreeves is to carry into execution the act for regulating swine. N. 464.

Appendix B

By this act--Any person who shall suffer his swine to go at large out of his inclosure, incurs a penalty of one shilling each, to be recovered with cost of suit by a hogreeve, or any other person who will sue for the same; of such swine may be impounded for the recovery of said penalty. But

Any town, at the annual meeting in March or April, may give liberty for swine to go at large, provided they be sufficiently yoked, from the 15th day of April to the 1st day of November, and constantly ringed in the nose all the time they shall be permitted to go at large.

A yoke accounted sufficient in law, must be the full depth of the swine's neck above the neck, and half so much below the neck, and the foal or bottom of the yoke full three times as long as the breadth or thickness of the swine's neck upon which it be placed.

The Power and Duty of a Pound Keeper (p. 131)

A pound keeper is to take care of the town's pound, to admit therein swine, sheep, horses, and neat cattle, liable by law to be impounded, and them therein to detain until the fees of the field driver, and his own fees be paid, and until the damages suffered by the person impounding them be paid by the owner thereof, with his fees, or until they be replevied, or sold as the law directs.

His fees are two pence per head for horses, and one penny for all sheep, and swine.

The Power and Duty of Field Drivers (p. 133)

1. Field drivers are to take up and impound any swine unyoked or unringed, horses unfettered, sheep not under the care of a shepherd, going at large on the common or highways leading through the town, between the fifteenth day of April, and the first day of November, and them in pound detain, or deal with, as is hereafter mentioned, until the owner shall pay for the use of the field driver, one shilling a head for all such horses, and three pence a head for all sheep and swine; besides two pence a head for all such horses, and one penny for all sheep and swine, to the pound keeper. . . .

2. If the owner of the creatures impounded, be unknown, the person impounding shall cause the same to be publickly cried, or notifications thereof as aforesaid posted up in some publick places in the town or district, and in the two next towns or districts adjoining, in case the distance thereunto from the place where the creatures may be taken up, doth not exceed four miles; and if no owner or claimer appear within three full days . . . the person so restraining them, may proceed with them in all respects, as the law provides respecting strays . . .

3. When the owner of the creatures impounded . . . shall think the damages mentioned in the memorandum left with the pound keeper are unreasonable, he may have the same ascertained by two or more disinterested judicious persons . . .

4. When an action of trespass shall be brought against the owner of any of the creatures aforesaid, for damages by them done upon his inclosed lands under improvement . . . the Justice or Court before whom the case shall be determined, may render judgment in favour of the person demanding damages for the injury sustained, upon satisfactory evidence being produced that such creatures were either clandestinely turned in, or broke into the close in a part where the fence was good and sufficient according to law . . .

The Power and Duty of a School Committee (p. 135)

1. It is the duty of the selectmen, or such committee as may be appointed to hire a schoolmaster, specially to attend to his morals -- and generally to employ such, and such only, as are qualified according to law, to discharge the duties thereby devolved upon them.

2. They are to use their influence and best endeavours that the youth of their town or district do regularly attend the schools appointed and supported for their instruction.

3. They shall once in every six months at least . . . visit and inspect the schools within their town . . . and enquire into the regulation and discipline thereof, and the proficiency of the scholars therein . . .

Appendix B

The Power and Duty of Inspectors of Nails (p. 138)

An inspector of nails is to open, thoroughly examine, and carefully inspect every cask of nails made for sale . . . and if he find the same made conformable to the assize and quality by law directed, to brand the same with the letters A.P. and the name of the town . . . and his own name . . .

The Power and Duty of Surveyors of Flax Seed (p. 140)

1. Surveyors of flaxseed are to inspect and survey all flaxseed that shall be intended to be laden on board of any vessel for exportation . . .

2. He may open the casks containing that commodity intended for exportation, and if need be, measure and shift the same into other casks, so as thoroughly to examine the whole, and see that it be clear from mixture of wild or other seed, or dirt, and of the measure aforesaid.

3. He shall mark or imprint with a burning iron, upon every cask . . . the letters A.P. with the name of the town . . . His own name at large, and the letter S at the end thereof.

4. He shall give to the owner or shipper of flaxseed shipped in bulk, by him examined and approved, a certificate of the quantity thereof.

The Power and Duty of an Inspector and Deputy Inspector of Pot and Pearl Ash (p. 142)

1. No person shall ship for exportation any pot or pearl ash before he submit the same to the view and examination of the inspector or his deputy, who shall start the same out of the casks, and carefully examine . . .

2. At the time of starting pot or pearl ash for inspection he shall weigh the cask or casks, and mark the weight with a marking iron on each head thereof.

3. He may by law, and without further or other warrant, enter on board any ship or vessel to inspect pot or pearl ash shipped . . . and if on search he shall discover any cask thereof, not branded, he may seize and secure the same . . .

Appendix B

The Power and Duty of Inspectors of Tobacco (p. 143)

1. An inspector of tobacco is to inspect all tobacco that shall be intended to be laden on board of any vessel for foreign exportation . . .

2. It is his duty to open the casks containing said commodity intended for exportation, and inspect it in four equal divisions . . . and see that it be properly dry, well cured, and not rotten or damaged, and of the weight, and packed in such casks as the law directs . . .

3. He shall mark or impress on every cask . . . with a burning iron, the letters A.P. -- the name of the town . . . his own name, and the letter I at the end thereof.

The Power and Duty of Provers of Butter in Firkins (p. 145)

1. It is their duty to inspect and prove all butter in firkins that shall be intended to be laden on board any vessel for exportation.

2. Every such prover is authorized to open the casks or firkins of such butter, and with a hollow iron searcher, perforate diagonally, from one side of the head of such cask to the other . . . and see that it be preserved with a due proportion of good fine salt, sweet and in all respects fit to be exported . . .

3. He shall mark every firkin of such butter . . . with a burning iron, with the letters A.P. - the name of the town . . . and his own name at large.

The Power and Duty of Inspectors of Loaf Sugar (p. 146)

They are to inspect all loaf sugar which is manufactured within the Commonwealth, and to be exported from the same by water, and give certificates of the weight . . .

Sources for Illustrations

_____. *Harmony Grove Cemetery, Salem, Mass.* (Salem, 1866) provided illustration on p. 126.

Abbott, John S.C. with Edward H. Elwell. *History of the State of Maine* (Augusta, 1892) provided illustration on p. 87.

Bickham, George. *The Universal Penman* (Dover Publications, 1968) provided illustration on p. 50.

Clark, George Faber. *A History of the Town of Norton* (Boston, 1859) provided illustrations on pp. 49 and 118.

Dana, Henry Swan. *History of Woodstock, Vermont* (Boston, 1889) provided illustration on p. 19.

Freeman, Samuel, *The Town Officer* . . . (Boston, 1793) photograph on p. 154 taken by Robert Shaw.

Grafton, Carol Belanger, ed. *Old-Fashioned Illustrations of Books, Reading, & Writing* (Dover Publications, 1992) provided illustration on p. 56.

Grafton, John, ed. *The American Revolution: A Picture Sourcebook* (Dover Publications, 1975) provided illustrations on pp. 20, 30, 77, 88, and 124.

Hornung, Clarence P., ed. *2000 Early Advertising Cuts* (Dover Publications, 1956) provided illustrations on pp. 12, 60, 63, 64, 73, 74, 82, 98, and 128.

McClintock, John N. *History of New Hampshire* (Boston, 1889) provided illustrations on pp. 121 and 134.

Munro, Wilfred H. *Picturesque Rhode Island* (Providence, 1881) provided illustrations on pp. 2 and 132.

Nevins, W.S. *Old Naumkeag: An historical sketch of the City of Salem* . . . (Salem, 1877) provided illustration on p. 78.

Rich, Shebnah. *Truro, Cape Cod or Land Marks and Sea Marks* (Boston, 1884) provided illustration on p. 36.

Sharpe, W.C. *History of Seymour, Connecticut* (Seymour, 1879) provided illustration on p. 46.

Teller, Daniel W. *The History of Ridgefield, Connecticut* (Danbury, 1878) provided illustrations on pp. 45, 55, and 81.

Town records of Deerfield, Massachusetts, provided illustrations on pp. 39-41, 66, and 69.

Town records of Reading, Massachusetts, provided illustrations on pp. 24 and 76.

Index to Persons

Index to Places

Ann Smith Lainhart has been a self-employed genealogist for the last fifteen years specializing in eastern Massachusetts research. She has also worked as a NEHGS reference librarian, and was editor of the Society's publication *First Boston City Directory (1789)*. Ms. Lainhart has published articles in both the *New England Historical and Genealogical Register* and *NEXUS*, as well as in *The American Genealogist* and the *National Genealogical Society Quarterly*. Her other publications include the books, *State Census Records*, and, as co-editor with Robert Dunkle, *New North Church Records*. She has done extensive transcriptions of the 1855 and 1865 Massachusetts State Census records for seventy- two towns. Ann Smith Lainhart is a member of the Association of Professional Genealogists and the Genealogical Speakers Guild. Currently, she and Robert Dunkle are preparing a book entitled *Boston Deaths 1700-1799*.